THE REAL
ROALD DAHL

For Harry and Felix

THE REAL
ROALD DAHL

Nadia Cohen

PEN & SWORD
HISTORY

AN IMPRINT OF PEN & SWORD BOOKS LTD.
YORKSHIRE - PHILADELPHIA

First published in Great Britain in 2018 by
PEN AND SWORD HISTORY
An imprint of
Pen & Sword Books Ltd
Yorkshire – Philadelphia

ISBN 978 1 52672 207 2

Printed and bound in the UK by TJ International Ltd,
Padstow, Cornwall
Typeset in Times New Roman 11/13.5 by
Aura Technology and Software Services, India

Pen & Sword Books Limited incorporates the imprints of Atlas, Archaeology,
Aviation, Discovery, Family History, Fiction, History, Maritime, Military, Military
Classics, Politics, Select, Transport, True Crime, Air World, Frontline Publishing,
Leo Cooper, Remember When, Seaforth Publishing, The Praetorian Press,
Wharncliffe Local History, Wharncliffe Transport, Wharncliffe True Crime and
White Owl.

For a complete list of Pen & Sword titles please contact
PEN & SWORD BOOKS LIMITED
47 Church Street, Barnsley, South Yorkshire, S70 2AS, England
E-mail: enquiries@pen-and-sword.co.uk
Website: www.pen-and-sword.co.uk

Or
PEN AND SWORD BOOKS
1950 Lawrence Rd, Havertown, PA 19083, USA
E-mail: Uspen-and-sword@casematepublishers.com
Website: www.penandswordbooks.com

Contents

Introduction

It's a name worthy of one of his strangest characters, but it is one known across the world as belonging to one of the most iconic, imaginative and masterful storytellers of all time. Generation after generation of children have fallen under the spell of Roald Dahl's *Fantastic*, *Marvellous* and *Revolting* tales, and they will continue to keep young readers giggling and gasping with glee for years to come.

The man was a genius when it came to creating less than perfect characters and he delighted in shining a light on the grotesque, the grisly, and the gruesome, but perhaps that was because he was so deeply flawed and complex himself. Roald could be boastful and brash; he was a bigot and a bully, an unfaithful husband and a tax dodger. But he was also a war hero, a romantic and a devoted father. He would go from being breathtakingly rude to devastatingly charming in a flash, from penny-pinching to incredibly generous with the vast fortune he made.

Although Roald always insisted that invention was far more interesting than reality, his own colourful life was as packed with as much high-octane drama as any of the stories he dreamt up in his vivid imagination. From narrowly surviving a harrowing plane crash as a young fighter pilot, to the tragically early death of his daughter, and a string of terrifying accidents and injuries which cursed his family, Roald was never far from another terrible twist of fate.

Born to Norwegian parents, he spent his childhood in rural Wales before losing his older sister and father in quick succession and being packed off to a traditional English boarding school where he was brutally beaten and utterly miserable. The highlight of his schooldays were the occasions when a nearby chocolate factory would send samples of new products for the pupils to test, leading this inquisitive young schoolboy to wonder just who could possibly be coming up with all these delicious ideas beyond the high walls.

In search of adventure after he left school, Roald joined the RAF to fight in the Second World War in North Africa and Greece as a Spitfire pilot. He narrowly survived crashing his plane over the Libyan desert, leaving him with crippling spinal injuries that would plague him for the rest of his life.

INTRODUCTION

Charming and debonair, he soon found himself being recruited by the government to promote British interests in Washington, where he made rich and powerful friends. His work took him to New York and Los Angeles but all he ever truly wanted was to write.

His high profile marriage to Hollywood starlet Patricia Neal was the subject of intense scrutiny, and although he was desperately in love with another woman for years, he nursed Patricia through the devastating aftermath of a terrible stroke. But the emotional torture which he endured after his 7-year-old daughter died haunted Roald for the rest of his life; the scars were so deep they never healed.

A string of unsuccessful operations on his back meant he was often cantankerous and difficult to deal with. His outspoken political opinions sparked widespread offence when he aired them publicly, and while he insisted his controversial views were misunderstood, accusations of racism and anti-Semitism continue to dog his memory today, almost thirty years after his death in November 1990 at the age of 74.

As a father of five, it was Roald's unique ability to truly understand children's minds that made him so extraordinarily successful. Roald craved the tranquillity of the English countryside, and was always happiest at Gipsy House, the beloved home in rural Buckinghamshire where he would see out his days. It was there he dreamt up the bedtime stories for his own children that would eventually become the inspiration for some of the most famous works in English literary history when he shut himself away for hours in his famous writing hut.

Little more than an unassuming shed at the bottom of the garden, insulated with foam tiles and reeking of tobacco, Roald would sit on a battered old armchair, with a green baize board over his lap, under the gloom of an ancient angle poise lamp. He always wrote in pencil on pages of lined yellow paper. A single bar electric heater hung from the ceiling, which he would poke with an old golf club if it played up. Even when he had become a millionaire many times over, he never bothered to replace it, and when the handle of his ancient filing cabinet broke off he replaced it with a piece of his own femur bone, which had been removed during one of his many operations.

Next to his armchair Roald kept not only a constant supply of chocolate bars and an enormous foil ball made of discarded sweet wrappers, but also a glass jar containing bits of his own spine, a macabre touch which was typical of the way he peppered his whimsical stories with gruesome and grisly touches. Indeed, some of his stories were so dark and the characters so deeply loathsome that he was – and still is – reviled by some librarians, parents and critics who fear he could bring out the worst in his readers.

But it is precisely these subversive and eccentric quirks which draw in his legions of loyal fans. Using his dynamic and surprising humour to such startling effect keeps readers entranced from the very first sentence.

The books speak for themselves and his literary legacy remains intact, but the man left behind a tangle of contradictions to unravel. He was a natural showman who guarded his privacy fiercely. He said he disliked the limelight but married a movie star. A large man, 6ft 6in tall, Roald was loud and theatrical; he loved to exaggerate wildly. He smoked and drank heavily, and had a ferocious temper; he insisted on strong opinions, and had no qualms about asking outrageously personal questions. He had a short fuse and would swear frequently and his outlook was often pessimistic, bleak, brutal and crass.

He married twice and suffered heartache, had an insatiable libido but insisted romance was nothing more than an a euphemism for sex, joking than no woman would get romantic with a eunuch and a castrated man was as much use as an aeroplane without an engine.

He adored listening to music, especially classical composers such as Stravinsky, but rarely watched live performances. He was an avid reader, but had little time for his fellow children's authors and was particularly dismissive of the likes of Dr Seuss, to whom he has often been compared. He said biographies were self-indulgent collections of facts – yet published two volumes of his own memoirs. He kept away from the London literary scene, living so close to his mother and three sisters in the Vale of Aylesbury that his daughter Tessa later nicknamed the area 'The Valley of the Dahls'. He insisted on saving money by growing his own vegetables and refused to make trans-Atlantic phone calls, but collected eye-wateringly expensive works of art.

He enjoyed cooking for friends but would make it abundantly clear the moment he was ready for guests to leave. He indulged in the finest wine money could buy – he loved Burgundy so much he was buried with several bottles from his cellar – but often embarrassed adults who came into his domain, challenging them to childish puzzles and games, or crucifying them over any political views they dared to express. Visitors recalled him holding court, always seated in his high-backed armchair at the head of the table where he feasted on expensive caviar, oysters and lobster, although lavish dinners always ended with cheap bars of chocolate. Not for Roald expensive truffles or liqueurs, this was a man who never grew out of the sweetshop favourites from his boyhood, and the character he most resembled was the one who remains a constant feature of our cultural conversation but was certainly no saint either, the notorious Mr Willy Wonka.

Chapter One

Roald Dahl was never remotely interested in his own ancestral past, turgid tales made up of a series of historical facts tended to bore him and he always urged his own relatives to look to the future, not the past. But had he delved back into his family tree he would have discovered some stories worthy of his own telling. He would have found that his great-grandfather, a Norwegian pastor called Iver Hesselberg, survived a massive fire that killed most of his congregation in 1822 by using a pile of Bibles to climb out of the window of his burning church.

Roald could also have learnt that his grandfather, Hans Theodor, trained for the priesthood and married into one of Norway's most distinguished families but was not as wise as his well-respected father, and recklessly gambled away the family's fortune. Theodor even dared to stake the village storehouse in a game of cards and when he lost the local community forced him out of his farm and he died penniless in 1898, leaving eleven children.

One of those children, Karl Laurits, studied science and law before moving to Oslo, then known as Christiania, where he married Ellen Wallace in 1884. Within a year the couple had a daughter, Sofie, who married a local butcher named Harald Dahl, one of six children. Shortly after their wedding, along with Harald's younger brother Oscar, the couple set sail in search of wider work opportunities. First they went to Paris, in the hope of living glamorous bohemian lives as painters, a passion Roald would later inherit as he often bought and sold expensive artworks to supplement his income when money was short. Roald was a lifelong gambler too, although his bets were not on the same scale as his grandfather.

Harald, Sofie and Oscar found it difficult to make ends meet in the French capital and so they went their separate ways. Oscar headed to La Rochelle where he lived as a fisherman, married a local French woman and even collaborated with the Nazis during the Second World War.

Harald meanwhile headed to Wales, having heard that there was lucrative work to be found in the coalmines of Cardiff. There were already well-established and successful trading relationships between Norway and Wales at the time, based on timber, steel and coal. Much of the coal being exported from Cardiff left on Norwegian-owned ships, so there were plenty of opportunities for entrepreneurial young men willing to work as shipbuilders, dockers or sailors. Harald is believed to have first arrived in Newport, fifteen miles further down the coast from Cardiff, in 1897 and soon found work and lodgings in Barry, but his heart remained in Paris where he had fallen in love with a glamorous woman fifteen years his junior called Marie Beaurin-Gressier. Three years later, having made enough money to impress her wealthy family, Harald returned to France and married her.

The newlyweds set up home together back in Cardiff and Harald build up a successful business with a close Norwegian friend, Ludvig Aadnesens, supplying ships with fuel, and trading coal. He and Marie had two children, Ellen born in 1903 and Louis in 1906, but while pregnant with their third child in 1907, Marie died at the age of just 29. Harald was devastated, and renamed their newly built house in the suburb of Llandaff Villa Marie in her honour. Alone with two young children at the age of 44, Harald found himself struggling to cope, even though Marie's mother had moved over from Paris to help. After four years he went to visit his sister Olga in Denmark, and was introduced to a family friend, 26-year-old Sofie Magdalene Hesselberg. Within weeks they were engaged, although her parents were certainly not keen on the idea of their daughter moving to Wales to raise another woman's children. They were soon married, enjoyed a romantic honeymoon in Paris, and hired a Norwegian nanny to help with the children, before returning to Wales together. The children were confused at suddenly being informed that they could no longer speak French as their mother had done, and initially there were tensions between Sofie Magdalene and her step-children.

Sofie, however, settled into her new life and within five years she had given birth to four children. Astri was born in 1912, followed by Alfhild in 1914 and then Roald on 13 September 1916, named after the famous Norwegian explorer Roald Amundsen who had successfully reached the South Pole in 1911. The following year, his younger sister Else joined the clan.

The Dahls were active members of the Norwegian Mission Church on a site overlooking the bay, which became a comforting reminder of home for over 75,000 seamen, and is now home to the Roald Dahl Millennium Centre. Officially, they were foreigners when the First World War broke out so the family had to apply for registration cards to live as aliens in Wales, causing some resentment between the two communities because Norway remained neutral throughout the conflict.

Learning two difficult languages simultaneously was challenging for Roald as a toddler, his parents insisted on speaking Norwegian at home, and he was slow to start to speak, but when he did his first words were a complete sentence. He apparently said in fluent Norwegian: 'Daddy, why aren't you wearing your slippers?'

With six happy, healthy and bilingual children, the Dahl family continued to prosper, and gradually started to move up in the world – to a sprawling farmhouse with 150 acres of land in the more affluent suburb of Radyr. The eldest children were dispatched to English boarding schools – Ellen to Rodean and Louis to Brighton College – and soon Sofie was pregnant once again.

At the start of 1920 Roald's infancy was struck by tragedy when his older sister Astri's appendix burst in the middle of the night. A doctor was summoned and performed emergency surgery on the table of their nursery, but the little girl never came round from the anaesthetic and a week later she died from an infection. She was only 7-years-old.

Astri was Harald's favourite child, according to her siblings, and her father was so overwhelmed by grief that he was struck dumb – he was literally speechless for days. And when he was taken ill with a bout of pneumonia a month later it was clear that Harald did not care if he lived or died. Roald wrote later: 'He was wanting to join her in heaven.' It was a feeling Roald would come to understand all too well years later when his own daughter also died suddenly at the age of 7.

Within six short weeks, Harald had his wish and died of pneumonia at the age of 57. He was buried next to his daughter, leaving Sofie not only bereft at the loss of her baby and her husband in rapid succession, but also having to care for Roald, his two sisters Alfhild and Else, as well as Harald's two children from his first marriage, Ellen and Louis. At the time her husband died Sofie was also pregnant with Roald's younger sister Asta, who was born in the autumn of 1920. She was 35, far from home and facing the daunting prospect of raising six children alone.

Chapter Two

Roald was just 3-years-old when his father died, and perhaps as a result he always found fatherhood a difficult subject himself. He had rocky relationships with his own children, particularly when they were teenagers, and when it came to his fictitious world, he often created children who had lost one or both parents – although he insisted that was merely a trick to win the reader's sympathy and had no bearing on his own experiences.

Like Roald himself, the children in his stories rarely appear to dwell much on their parents' deaths. In *The BFG* when Sophie, the little girl growing up in a dreary orphanage, was asked if she missed her parents she replied: 'Not really, because I never knew them.'

Roald never really knew his father either, but was endlessly fascinated by hearing stories about him. Harald had lost an arm following an accident at the age of 14 – it had been amputated unnecessarily after a drunken doctor misdiagnosed a dislocated shoulder. Roald delighted in retelling how his father learnt to do everything one-handed, except cutting the top off a hard boiled egg, a trick he could never quite seem to master. Although he had very few real memories of Harald, in Roald's vivid imagination, his father was a glamorous and romantic figure who heroically triumphed over every adversity to carve out a better life for his family. By the time he died Harald had amassed a fortune, the equivalent of around £5 million today, although Sofie had very little control over the money she inherited, and before spending it she always had to seek approval from his brother and his business partner who were the trustees of the estate.

Soon after Sofie gave birth to Asta, she decided to sell the rather isolated farm in rural Radyr, along with all the animals and servants, and returned to the Norwegian community in Llandaff. It was not easy for Sofie as a single mother, but she never had a bad word to say about Harald and over the years she cheerfully helped embellish the myths about him which Roald passed on to his own children in time. Roald did however forge a close relationship with his paternal grandfather Olaus, who died in 1923 at the age of 89, having already made quite an impression on his young grandson. Roald inherited his height from Olaus, who he later described as 'an amiable giant almost seven foot tall,' and who was said by some to have inspired the character of the good natured giant in *The BFG*.

When the Dahls moved back to Llandaff they no longer had the servants Harald had insisted upon, but the family did have a gardener, Mr Jones, who the children called Joss. They all adored him but, growing up in a house full of girls, Roald was particularly fond of him. Joss became something of a father figure after Olaus died and would take Roald to watch his beloved Cardiff City football club play, inspiring a lifelong love of the game. Roald later recalled how standing in the crowds, cheering on the team, gave him 'an almost unbearable sense of thrill and rapture'.

Most of Roald's characters seemed to survive without much in the way of practical or emotional support from their parents, and in an interview Roald claimed that most children felt ignored by their parents and viewed them as 'the enemy'. In *Charlie and the Chocolate Factory*, little Charlie Bucket's closest ally was neither of his parents, but his Grandpa Joe, and in *The Witches*, the orphaned narrator's closest relationship is with his Norwegian grandmother. Matilda Wormwood, from *Matilda*, has awful parents too – vulgar caricatures who try to stop their daughter reading. In *James and The Giant Peach*, James is left to the care of his wicked aunts and understandably prefers insects to humans. Dahl's own memoir of his childhood, *Boy*, is a series of colourful impressions and sketchy flashbacks which reveal his mastery of storytelling, rather than an accurate account of his youth. Each anecdote was fleshed out with fictitious elements, although Roald once insisted: 'Some are funny, some are painful. Some are unpleasant. All are true.' To help his recollection when he wrote *Boy* in his old age, Roald reread the archive of 906 letters he had sent to his mother which were preserved carefully throughout her own life and his. He adored Sofie and once he settled in Great Missenden he bought her a house just a few minutes walk away, where she lived until the end of her life.

Despite his disparaging attitude towards mother figures in his stories, Roald credited his own mother with inspiring many of his life's great passions, including cookery, art and gardening. He praised her for being practical and fearless often to the point of recklessness when it came to her children, taking them on action packed adventures and entertaining them with fabulous tales she dreamt up. She loved to gossip until well into her old age, and Roald clearly inherited his love of storytelling from his mother as well as a strong desire for wild flights of exaggeration which never really left him. Roald's second autobiography, *Going Solo*, also included scores of made up details peppered with elaborate embellishments.

His parents heritage was important to Roald and he always felt a strong affinity for it, perhaps in part due to his mother never renouncing her Norwegian nationality despite living in Britain for more than fifty years. Being foreign caused her great problems during both world wars, when she was officially forced to live as an alien, but even that was not enough to change her mind. Although she spoke and wrote English, Sofie made sure that all four of her children learned her mother tongue fluently and took them to Norway every summer holiday to visit her relatives. Years later Roald would describe those trips as 'totally idyllic', adding: 'The mere mention of them used to send shivers of joy rippling all over my skin.' He frequently took his own children on summer holidays to Norway too.

Roald occasionally described Norway as home, but when he was in Africa serving as a pilot during the Second World War, and again when posted in America, it was not the fjords of Norway or the Welsh valleys, but rural England that he found himself pining for. He would certainly have thought of himself as British, and he was a British citizen from birth, but throughout his schooldays Roald was known by the other boys as 'the foreigner'.

The first school he attended was a local nursery called Elm Tree House, run by two sisters, Mrs Corfield and Miss Tucker, before moving on to Llandaff Cathedral School when he was 7. He attended the all boys school from September 1923 until 1925, during which time he and his friends staged an elaborate prank on the bad tempered local sweetshop owner Mrs Pratchett. The trick, which would later become well known as The Great and Daring Mouse Plot, involved the boys distracting the miserable shopkeeper while Roald slipped a dead mouse into a jar of sweets while she was not looking. She was so shocked when she opened the glass jar and saw the mouse, which the boys had discovered under the floorboards at school, that she dropped the sweets in horror and the glass smashed on the ground. Roald was immensely pleased with himself: 'We all have our moments of brilliance and glory, and this was mine,' he wrote with glowing pride in *Boy*.

The sweetshop now bears an historic blue plaque in honour of the prank. At the time the village sweetshop was the most important place in the world to the boys, and as far as they could tell, the repulsive Mrs Pratchett was the most evil woman in the world. Roald described her as looking like many vicious hags he would eventually come to create. Mrs Pratchett was: 'A skinny old hag with a moustache on her upper lip and a mouth as sour as a green gooseberry.'

But Mrs Pratchett was furious at the prank, and even though Roald and his friends had scarpered, she soon tracked down who was responsible and demanded they were punished immediately with a caning from the headmaster Mr Coombes. Roald vividly remembered being spanked on the bottom but from the moment he started to describe the pain he endured, the story instantly stopped being funny. Roald recalled being struck so hard 'that it emptied my lungs of every breath of air that was in them. It is bad enough when the cane lands on fresh skin, but when it comes down on bruised and wounded flesh it is unbelievable.'

Roald's mother was horrified when she saw the marks on her son's backside that evening, she thought corporal punishment was a completely unsuitable way to discipline a child, and took him out of the school at the end of that term. Roald was just 9-years-old when he was sent away from home for the first time, to a boarding school called St Peter's, in Somerset, which he later said was like 'a private lunatic asylum', and the beatings from the headmaster were just as frequent and vicious as they had been at Llandaff Cathedral School. The headmaster kept a large collection of canes in his office, and appeared to enjoy beating his pupils.

Roald hated being thrown into a male dominated environment, where the only female was the matron whom he thought 'disliked small boys very much indeed'. He was desperately homesick, and would lie in his uncomfortable bed miserably gazing out across the Bristol Channel towards the family and beloved pet mice Marmaduke and Montague he had left behind. Once he even faked the symptoms of appendicitis in a bid to be sent home, knowing it was the illness that had killed his sister.

Although he struggled academically, Roald gradually began to settle into life at the new school, largely because he was tall for his age, which made him an asset to the rugby, football and cricket teams. He started showing early signs of enterprise, and earned extra cash by selling kerosene in the villages surrounding Midsomer Norton. Roald also started doing crossword puzzles and devising his own word games, a skill which would later serve him so well.

It was at this time that he started to write home regularly, always signing his letters 'Boy', a nickname he used because of living in a house full of women and girls. He did not start using his real name in letters until he was 10. He also began to develop a love of reading, and his favourite books were always the ones that made him laugh the most, including Hilaire Belloc's *Cautionary Verses*, poems about naughty children who often meet grisly deaths, which he learned off by heart. Soon he had moved on to more typically adventurous stories such as *The Jungle Book* by Rudyard Kipling and Robert Louis Stevenson's *Treasure Island*. Later he started to prefer wartime spy thrillers like *Secret of the Baltic* by T. C. Bridges and *The Spy In Black* by J. Storer Clouston, and imagined what it might be like to be a wartime flying ace. He also developed a fascination with Gothic horror and ghost stories, and recalled being so petrified by the ghoulish tales in Ambrose Bierce's *Can Such Things Be?* that he had to sleep with the light on.

But the stories that stayed in his memory and influenced him the most were the dark tales his mother would tell him, adapted from ancient Norwegian fables, about mythical and grotesque creatures, such as *The Hare Who Laughed Until His Jaws Cracked* and *The Boy Who Challenged A Troll to an Eating Competition*, characters he found he could easily envision.

Sofie left Wales and moved the family to Bexley in Kent, into a large house called Oakwood which boasted two acres of grounds and even a billiard room where Roald developed a passion for the sport which became such an integral part of his life that his beloved snooker cues were among the collection of items placed beside Roald in his grave.

They still returned to Wales for regular holidays, carefree days which Roald longed for more than ever after he was packed off to another remote boarding school in 1930, at the age of 13. Repton School near Derby was 130 miles north of Bexley and Roald pleaded to stay at home, but Sofie was keeping the promise she had made to Roald's late father to ensure all the children received a traditional English education. Roald found the elaborate school uniform of a frock coat and straw boater hat quite ridiculous, and he was equally baffled by many of the new customs, rules and rituals he was expected to learn and abide by. He slept, ate and studied at The Priory, one of the nine boarding houses, where he had to work out how he was expected to fit into the rigid hierarchy which included 'boazers' – school slang for older boys who wielded all the power, and treated the younger boys as their servants, or 'fags'. As soon as Roald arrived he became the 'bim fag' – the most junior fag who in turn had to be shown the ropes by the 'tip fag', a boy in his second year.

As the lowest in the social pecking order, Roald's tasks included anything from warming cold toilet seats – to Roald's horror the lavatories did not have doors on them – to cleaning, keeping the fire lit, polishing the older boys' shoes and occasionally even cooking meals for them. But there were also far more torturous and humiliating rituals which included the younger boys being stripped naked and whipped with wet towels, or having chewing gum rubbed into their pubic hair.

Roald knew he was stuck at Repton until the age of 18 and the long years stretched ahead of him like a prison sentence. From the very start he was deeply unhappy, lonely and resentful. He survived in a state of constant terror of being either cruelly bullied by other boys or viciously whipped by sadistic masters. It was a time when punishing children with a cane or strap was routine. In *Boy* he wrote:

> Our lives at school were quite literally ruled by fear of the cane. We walked in the knowledge that if we put a foot wrong, the result would be a beating. It is clear to me now, although it wasn't at the time, that these boys had developed this curiously detached attitude towards these vile tortures in order to preserve their sanity. It was an essential defensive mechanism. Had they crowded round and commiserated with me and tried to comfort me, I think we would have all broken down.

Roald longed to escape but never actually tried to run away, and managed to find ways to survive, perhaps having already been hardened by his experiences at St Peter's, and again it helped that he was very good at sport. But when it came to the classroom, Roald found the lessons dull and repetitive. His academic reports were usually poor, accusing him of 'childishness, idleness, apathy and stupidity'. His teachers were frustrated by what they saw as his overly imaginative use of language, as well as his absurd humour and anarchic writing style. A former contemporary of Roald's, David Atkins, said he once told him: 'Life isn't beautiful and sentimental and clear. It's full of foul things and horrid people and incidentally, rhyming is old hat.'

For Roald, the absolute highlight of his school career by far was when the marketing department of the nearby Cadbury's chocolate factory wanted to test out new products before they were launched. Each pupil was sent a box of chocolate bars from the factory, along with a form to give their opinions. Roald took this tasting job exceptionally seriously, and supplied detailed feedback. He never forgot the thrill of the moment new boxes arrived, and he imagined working in the factory to be the most exciting thing he could think of. Of course this is what inspired his most famous story, *Charlie and the Chocolate Factory*, the story of a little boy called Charlie Bucket, who wins the chance to tour a mysterious local factory run by the elusive and eccentric inventor Willy Wonka. Roald decided then to invent a fantasy world for himself and set about creating an alternative existence in his frequent letters home, partly to reassure his mother that he was not completely miserable, but also to keep himself entertained. His writing from that point on was sprinkled with comical details, wild exaggerations and vivid descriptions, once saying a Matron had 'Hair like a fuzzie-wuzzie and two warts on her face.'

Roald was desperately homesick, and endured hours alone, but after a couple of years life at Repton became a little more tolerable when he was no longer a fag and struck up a close friendship with an older boy called Michael Arnold. Roald called Michael 'the cleverest boy in England', and together they explored the surrounding countryside, conducted elaborate experiments and shared a mutual fascination with photography – spending long hours in the school darkroom developing their prints. All their spare pocket money was spent on photographic paper or gramophone records. Michael was the only boy Roald ever referred to by his first name, and he was soon invited to join the Dahls for Christmas in Bexley, and later on their annual summer holiday to Norway. He became part of the family, but in May 1933 Roald sent his mother some shocking news: 'Michael has had a severe mental breakdown and has had to go away for the rest of the term before he goes to Oxford,' he wrote. It later emerged that Michael had in fact been expelled for homosexual activity with some younger boys, but their housemaster S. S. Jenkyns, known to the boys as Binks, wrote to Sofie assuring her at length that Roald had not been involved.

Jenkyns explained:

> It was a very unpleasant business for everybody and especially for Roald; not only because he lost his chief friend, but also because people were likely to think that he was implicated. But as a matter of fact there was no sort of suspicion attaching to him, in fact I am convinced that he had done his best to make Arnold give up his bad ways; but the latter is very obstinate and would not listen to him.

Roald later admitted to his mother that he had known the truth all along, but had agreed to go along with the pretext of a mental breakdown – which had been Arnold's father's preferred version of events – to save his friend any public humiliation. In another letter home Roald wrote: 'I knew that he had a kink about him. I tried to stop him, as Binks knew, but it was no good.'

Before his expulsion, Michael had been further punished by the headmaster with a beating so brutal that it left blood pouring from his naked buttocks; it was thought that the headmaster at the time was Geoffrey Fisher, who went on to become the Archbishop of Canterbury. However, when *Boy* was published years later it turned out that the incident had actually occurred a year after Fisher had left the school and a new headmaster was in place.

Roald and Michael stayed very close friends for more than fifty years, during which Michael became a respected scientist, married and had three children. Roald was astonished when he sent one of his own sons back to Repton. While other pupils later recounted various incidents of sexual abuse at Repton, Roald's great height seemed to have made him immune to unwanted advances. Needless to say, girls were in short supply, and pupils at Repton were not given much in the way of sex education, although Roald often delighted in retelling a humorous anecdote about a teacher warning boys about the danger of masturbation. It was suggested that, like torches, their penises only had a limited power supply, and the boys were instructed 'not to touch it or the batteries will go flat'.

After Michael was expelled, Roald found himself alone again and spent his spare time travelling the Derbyshire countryside on the secret motorcycle that his mother had given him, which he had to keep hidden from the masters in the barn of a nearby farm. He had no interest in going to university, all he craved was adventure, foreign travel and getting as far away from Repton as he possibly could. His final school report read: 'If he can master himself, he will become a leader.'

Sofie was frantic with worry about what his future held, so sent Roald to see a psychic who apparently predicted, with remarkable accuracy, that he was going to become a writer.

Chapter Three

The moment he was allowed to escape the narrow confines of boarding school Roald began his frantic search for excitement and freedom. He joined the Public School Exploring Society when he turned 18, eagerly signing up for a trip to map Nova Scotia on foot.

The group eagerly began their four-week journey from Liverpool to Newfoundland off the coast of Canada a few weeks after their final term was over in 1934. Roald was the official photographer of the twelve-man crew. What sounded like a fun and daring escapade soon plunged the boys into a gruelling test of their endurance as the hiking conditions were far tougher than any of them had anticipated. Exhausted, cold and hungry, a dozen ill-prepared teenagers found themselves wading through deep mosquito infested swamps by day and struggling to sleep in leaking tents at night: 'Honestly I don't think any one of us has ever been so miserable,' Roald wrote in his diary.

He soon realised he could not stand their leader, Surgeon Commander Admiral George Murray Levick, who horrified the entire camp by defecating in front of them every morning. Roald felt the man in charge was putting them all in unnecessary danger and abandoned the expedition at the first opportunity. When he returned to England, Roald realised he had no choice but to get a job, although he did not have the first clue what he wanted to do. He enjoyed writing but there was no chance of making a career out of that and since nothing else particularly appealed to him he hunted around for the sort of role which sounded like there might be some potential for future travel – or even just a chance of meeting girls.

He quickly landed his first job in the accounts department of the Asiatic Petroleum Company in the city of London, earning £130 a year, but Roald was bored out of his mind from the very start. One thing was abundantly clear, he was not cut out for the daily grind of office life or the drudgery of a crowded commute in and out of the capital every day.

CHAPTER THREE

He told a friend: 'I went into oil because all girls go for oilmen,' but the accountancy work was dull, and all he could think about was planning his next adventure. He longed to be sent to an exotic location such as Africa or Mexico, but since he was still not yet a British national he was stuck in the UK for several more years. Roald tried to make the best of his four years in suburbia. He kept himself busy with various hobbies; he carried on with his photography and set up a darkroom in his mother's sprawling Edwardian mansion in Kent, took up golf and started regularly attending a local greyhound dog racing track, beginning a lifelong love of gambling. He had secretive affairs with a couple of married women who lived locally, seeming to enjoy the drama and the intrigue, until he finally met a girl his own age. Dorothy O' Hara Livesay was his first girlfriend, but soon after they started dating, Roald finally got his wish and was posted abroad. There was no contest and the thought of staying at home appears not to have occurred to him for a moment. Dorothy, known as Dolly, tearfully waved her boyfriend off to East Africa in September 1938, but within a few months of his leaving she had married one of his friends.

Roald never looked back. This was what he had been waiting for. At 22-years-old he was the most junior member of the team joining the Shell Oil Terminal in Dar es Salaam, but Roald was finally about to see the world. As he set off on the two-week voyage to Tanzania, Roald felt his life was beginning at last. And what an adventure it was. Shell had arranged for luxurious Colonial-style accommodation for the staff and Roald found he had been assigned a spacious villa close to the beach. The climate may have been so stiflingly hot that he needed to take four baths a day, but Roald loved his foreign new environment which was a world away from the rainy streets of London he had loathed so much. Everything was unfamiliar and new. He wrote home gleefully exclaiming: 'There were no furled umbrellas, no bowler hats, no sombre grey suits and I never once had to get on a train or a bus.'

It was the dying days of the British Empire, a whirlwind of cocktail parties and decadence, and although he did not think much of his new colleagues, Roald threw himself wholeheartedly into his new expatriate life. He had his own cook and several personal servants catering for his every whim. Eager to fit in, he became an active member of the Dar es Salaam Club, wore crisp white suits every day, played squash, darts and golf, and developed a taste for strong 'sundowner' cocktails each evening. Roald struck up a great friendship with one of his servants, Mdisho, who loyally woke him each morning with tea and an orange, ran his bath and laid out his fresh clothes for the day. Years later, when Roald first drew sketches of Charlie Bucket, the hero of *Charlie and the Chocolate Factory*, he was a young black boy based on Mdisho.

Roald filled his frequent letters home with scores of colourful anecdotes about the hilarious characters he encountered at boozy ex-pat parties, his encounters with black mambas, lions and the various new pets he adopted including a pair of lizards called Hitler and Mussolini. He seemed to enjoy sending the family frequent updates about his bowel movements, which he described in great detail. His letters were also full of unflattering remarks about the local African people, he once complained: 'They're all the same, these bloody Hindus.' He also wrote about 'their thousands of bloody relations'; 'no less than eight horrible little naked children' and 'blokes with nothing on except a bit of coconut matting.'

For the final few months of his posting, Roald moved out of the shared villa and lived alone for the first time in his life. It was a daunting prospect after being looked after by his mother, sisters and school staff for so long, but Roald relished his new-found independence. He was thrilled to have the chance to blast his records at full volume, manage his domestic staff in the way he wanted, and best of all to choose his own menus. Being allowed to decide what to eat at mealtimes, and working out what time they should be served, was a completely novel experience for him.

But news of the outside world seeped in and since it looked increasingly likely that Britain was on the brink of war, Roald worried constantly about his mother and sister. When the Second World War broke out in 1939, he urged them repeatedly to move back to the safety of Wales, fearing that Bexley was directly under the flight path of the German bomber planes that would soon be making their way to London. Roald had happy memories of their family holidays in Tenby and he thought it made sense for the family to decamp there until the danger passed, but Sofie stubbornly refused to go as she was convinced the war would be over in a matter of weeks. But when Roald heard that the Battle of Britain was beginning, with London coming under increasing fire, he urged his sister Else's fiancé, an RAF pilot, to try to explain how much danger they were in. But still they were all determined to wait it out and remain in Kent. He wrote: 'You've no right to be sitting in one of the most dangerous places in the world at the moment, quite happy in the mere thought that you've got a cellar. That cellar's no good once the real raids start.'

On 7 September 1940, the skies over Bexley darkened dramatically as German bombers swarmed towards London, attacking the East End docks and Woolwich Arsenal in one of the longest and most devastating attacks of the Blitz. Sofie, Else, Asta and their seven dogs sheltered in the cellar for the next ten days – with little to do but drink the champagne, wine and cognac that lined the walls. But eventually they were forced out by the Army, who requisitioned the large house as an officer's mess. They were given just twelve hours to find alternative accommodation, so Sofie urgently contacted her eldest daughter Alfhild who was by then living in Buckinghamshire with her husband Leslie Hansen. Since none of Roald's family had British passports, and they had a large number of pets in tow, their options were limited, but Alfhild found them a cottage in a nearby village called Ludgershall.

As a foreign national Sofie still had to report to the police every week while Alfhild became a Land Girl, helping boost agricultural production when many farm workers had been conscripted to join the armed forces, and Asta joined the Women's Auxiliary Air Force as a radio operator.

Thousands of miles away in Tanzania, the British forces were rounding up the hundreds of Germans living in Dar es Salaam. Roald decided he should do his bit to help the war effort and enlisted as a Special Constable with the King's African Rifles, a platoon of indigenous Askari men whose job it was to arrest any Germans attempting to escape across the border, and take them to internment camps which were being set up by the British authorities.

Roald managed the unpleasant task he was set with some success, but disliked seeing Dar es Salaam filling with soldiers and wanted to escape the city too. He decided to join the Royal Air Force as a pilot, since the Army did not appeal to him. Roald felt sure that flying would be preferable to marching in the heat; days later he drove the 600 miles overland to Nairobi to enrol at the Initial Training School, and was accepted to begin flight training straight away, along with sixteen other men.

Roald was issued with the service number 774022, but at 6ft 6in tall, they found he struggled to squeeze into his tiny two seater De Haviland Tiger Moth plane. With his head poking up above the windshield it was difficult for him to breathe, but from the start, Roald loved flying and was one of the best students. After just seven hours and forty minutes experience in the air he was allowed to fly solo; he never forgot the thrilling sensation and often talked of the joy he felt being able to watch the wildlife as he soared above the African plains. Roald quickly graduated on to an advanced flying course in RAF Habbaniya, fifty miles west of Baghdad in Iraq, where he was given six months training on Hawker Hart planes – waking before dawn to fly early each morning before the temperatures reached a sweltering fifty degrees – and studying navigation, meteorology and technical skills in the afternoons.

Roald was appalled at the poverty that surrounded the airbase in Baghdad, which he described as 'a bloody awful town', but found he was equally fascinated and surprised by the racial diversity. He wrote: 'The pavements are simply packed with every conceivable kind of person – Arabs, Syrians, Jews, Negroes, Indians and the majority who are just nothing at all, with faces the colour of milk chocolate, and long flowing, but very dirty robes.'

After completing his training, having logged 150 flying hours, he was officially commissioned as a pilot officer on 24 August 1940. He was commended for working hard and, having thoroughly enjoyed the course, he was among the top trainees. Roald finished third out of forty candidates in the final exams and passed with a special distinction. Whether he was prepared for it or not he was being sent to join an RAF squadron and face the enemy. Roald had no idea what lay ahead but there was no turning back. He was going to war.

Dispatched alongside the sixteen other young pilots recruited with him earlier in the year, Roald was assigned to No 80 Squadron, and together they flew directly into the Allied frontlines of the North African Desert, but Roald would be one of only three to survive the war. The young men had not actually been given any air-to-air combat training, and the long hours they spent in tiny cockpits, often flying through desert sandstorms, left them shaking with exhaustion.

19 September 1940 was his first day as a combat pilot, and Roald was instructed to fly an unfamiliar light bomber aircraft, The Gloster Gladiator, from an airstrip at Abu Sueir on the Suez Canal in Egypt to a squadron waiting at a secret location. He was excited about the challenge which he would make by stages.

The first stop, in the middle of a sandstorm swirling over the Libyan desert, was another small airstrip where he was to refuel his plane and find out the coordinates of where he was headed next. The officer showed him on a map a tiny town which he should be able to reach within fifty minutes, before darkness fell. Roald's final destination was 80 Squadron's forward airstrip thirty miles south of Mersa Matruh and he took off immediately.

Roald knew it was dangerous since the airstrip would be camouflaged, the light was beginning to fade, and with no cloud cover, weather conditions were notoriously unpredictable in the desert and could change suddenly. After fifty minutes in the air, with the sun setting, there was no sign of an airstrip, nor any tents; no habitation of any sort. Roald began to panic and, running dangerously low on fuel, realised he was left with no choice but to attempt an emergency landing in the middle of nowhere and pray that a search party would find him in the morning. He was forced to land his plane at 80mph in the pitch darkness, but the undercarriage of his plane hit a rock and he crashed. The front of the aircraft was pushed into the ground, throwing him forward. He fractured his skull, smashed his nose and was temporarily blinded.

Minutes after the crash the plane's fuel tanks exploded, but luckily the strong smell of petrol roused him and although the blast had left Roald numb, he somehow managed to force the canopy open before dragging himself from the blazing wreckage and collapsing onto the sand outside, slumping into unconsciousness just moments before the plane burst into flames and was completely destroyed. Barely conscious and in excruciating pain, Roald managed to crawl away from the fire, but was not out of danger. The heat from the crash caused the eight machine guns to start firing off more than fifty rounds of ammunition, and bullets showered down around him from all directions. He recalled later: 'My face hurt most. I slowly put a hand up to feel it. It was very sticky. My nose didn't seem to be there. I tried to feel my teeth to see if they were still there, but it seemed as through one or two were missing.'

Miraculously, none of the bullets actually hit him, and he passed out again minutes later. A second stroke of luck was that three infantrymen had seen the plane come down and set off to search for the body of the pilot. When they found Roald among the wreckage they were astounded to discover he was still breathing. His face and overalls were so badly burnt that at first they wrongly identified him as an enemy Italian pilot when he reached the Ambulance Station in Mersah Matruh. He soon regained consciousness, but not his eyesight, and was transferred by train to the Royal Navy Anglo Swiss Hospital in Alexandria. For weeks Roald was unable to open his eyes and doctors feared he would be left permanently blind. He was in complete darkness for over a month, concussed and confused about what the future might hold for him. He spent almost six months in hospital, at first sleeping for over sixteen hours a day; gradually, he started to recover. After weeks of total darkness his eyesight returned and his facial features were carefully reconstructed by a top Harley Street plastic surgeon who had joined the army.

Over the weeks he fell in love with one of the nurses who cared for him, Mary Welland, and she was by his side when he first opened his eyes, bathed them for an hour each day and talked to him. She sparked a lifetime of respect and admiration for the nursing profession.

Roald soon discovered that the RAF inquiry into his crash revealed that he had been given the completely wrong location and had mistakenly been sent into the dangerous no-man's land between the Allied and Italian forces. He was also given the distressing news that his home in Bexley had been hit by German bombers, although his mother and sisters had escaped with their lives. The fact that they had all somehow managed to survive made Roald focus on what really mattered to him, and it helped him stay calm in the face of uncertainty.

He reflected later that he had not actually been particularly frightened at the prospect of never being able to see again, only that he might lose his family: 'Blindness, not to mention life itself, was no longer too important,' he wrote. 'The only way to conduct oneself in a situation where bombs rained down and bullets whizzed past was to accept all the dangers and all the consequences as calmly as possible. Fretting and sweating about it all was not going to help.'

His injuries had been so severe that doctors wanted to send Roald home – he was in agony and had not seen his family for two years – but he insisted on staying near the base in the hope that he might one day be allowed to fly again. When he was finally discharged from hospital, Roald spent all his savings on gold watches for each of the nurses who had cared for him, and was sent to Alexandria to convalesce with Teddy and Dorothy Peel, a wealthy English couple who opened their lavish home to injured officers. He was still very weak, severely underweight, suffering debilitating headaches and often had trouble concentrating, but the Peels and their staff rallied around to help restore his strength.

Roald longed to be reunited with his squadron, who by then had been moved from North Africa to Greece, and he was determined to put the crash behind him and prove his worth as a fighter pilot. He did not want the others to think he was not up to the job, although it had been made clear that the accident was not his fault since he was not given adequate training in a Gloster Gladiator plane, only in a similar Gloster Gauntlet, and the commanding officer had given him the wrong coordinates for the landing strip. For years he delighted in retelling the anecdote, portraying himself as the heroic flying ace, usually embellishing the dramatic story further by claiming that he had been 'shot down' in combat over the North African desert, and never pointing out that his plane had run out of fuel. When retelling the incident, as he did in both *Shot Down Over Libya* and

A Piece of Cake, Roald also failed to mention that there had actually been a second pilot with him that night. In Roald's version of events, he cheated death and fought desperately for his life alone – and was lucky to have been discovered by the infantrymen who saw his plane coming down – but it has since emerged that in fact Douglas McDonald was flying alongside him from Fouka in another Gladiator plane, and when he saw what happened he landed his plane safely nearby. Many years later Roald admitted that Douglas had stayed with him in his hour of need, comforting him through the night until help arrived at dawn. The two men forged such a close bond that long dark night that they even came up with affectionate nicknames for one another – Roald was known as Lofty, while McDonald, who had grown up in Africa, was Shorty. Although he was later erased from Roald's much more colourful version of events, McDonald has since described that night as the worst of his life – he had risked his own survival by choosing to stay with his friend, since they knew the Italian enemy was not far away.

Many years later McDonald did die in a plane crash and in a touching letter sent to his widow after his death, Roald finally revealed the whole truth about what had taken place between them that fateful night. It was the first time he had admitted how vulnerable he actually felt in the immediate aftermath of the Gloster coming down: 'I doubt he explained how really marvellous he was to me, and looked after me and tried to comfort me, and stayed with me out there during a very cold night, and kept me warm,' Roald wrote.

All the doctors who examined him had been highly pessimistic that Roald would ever return to active service. His injuries were still healing, with occasionally erratic bouts of light-headedness and forgetfulness, which made it an unlikely prospect that he could be trusted to take control of the cockpit of a plane. While he had been convalescing with the Peels, Roald became a part of the thriving expatriate social scene, playing rounds of golf and bridge, and occasionally joining them at colonial cocktail parties where his outspoken and often outrageous views made him a popular guest. During this time he met his next proper girlfriend, a friend of his sister's called Lesley Pares, whom he liked immediately because she seemed blissfully unaffected by his fierce political arguments – which were liberally punctuated with swear words. Staring death in the face seemed to leave Roald with even more confidence than before, he felt he had been given a second chance at life. He loved to shock, particularly when he was among genteel society, and was rarely embarrassed, which amused Lesley and attracted her to him enormously. Shortly after their first meeting Roald enthusiastically wrote home to his mother describing his new flame as 'much nicer than the average Judy one meets here – most of them are bloody awful.'

But by February 1941, feeling stronger and no longer suffering the blackouts he had endured on and off since the accident, Roald was passed fully fit for flying duties again, having previously only been allowed back on light duties at the RAF base near Cairo, mostly delivering messages around the city. He had desperately hoped to return to flying one day, he missed the sense of freedom and isolation. He never forgot the glorious feeling that flying had given him, all too briefly, and it was a theme which he would revisit in many of his future novels. In several of his most famous stories including *The Minpins* and *James and the Giant Peach* small boys escaped their troubles and tormentors by flying away.

While Lesley had provided a welcome distraction while he was on light duties, Roald still had his sights very firmly set on getting back into the air, and seven months after his accident when the call came giving him the chance to rejoin his colleagues for additional flight training, Roald leapt at it. By this time 80 Squadron had been transferred to the Greek campaign based at RAF Ismailia in Eleusina, near Athens. They were now equipped with Hawker Hurricanes, the battered old Gloster Gladiators were no longer in use, and Roald would be taught to fly a brand new Mark 1 Hurricane although he had trouble folding himself into that one too.

Despite his physical failings, in April 1941, following a short refresher course which had only actually seen him take to the air for around seven hours, Roald was told he would be flying to Greece as part of the Allied forces campaign to resist the strength of the Nazi invasion. The odds were stacked against them, as the British and Greek pilots were far outnumbered by the German Luftwaffe. The RAF only had a total of eighteen combat aircraft in Greece: fourteen Hurricanes and four Bristol Blenheim light bombers.

Roald was understandably wracked with nerves as he rejoined 80 Squadron who were preparing to embark upon what looked like another doomed mission. 'I had no experience at all flying against the enemy,' he wrote later,

> I had never been in an operational squadron. And now they wanted me to jump into a plane I had never flown in before and fly it to Greece to fight against a highly efficient air force that outnumbered us by a hundred to one. The thought that I might

never get out of the country alive didn't occur to me. It should
have done, and looking back on it now I am surprised that it didn't.

On 15 April 1941 Roald found himself flying high over the city of Chalcis,
where German Junkers Ju-88 planes were bombing ships. Roald shot one
down and returned to the base, realising he had probably just killed a man.
The next day in another air battle he shot down a second Ju-88, killing
another German pilot. Two days later Roald joined a third dramatic aerial
dogfight which later became known as the Battle of Athens, alongside
the high scoring British Second World War ace Pat Pettle, and his friend
David Coke. The Allied squadron was the underdog, underprepared and
vastly outnumbered by the Germans, their chances of survival looked
slim. Roald later described it as 'A long and beautiful dogfight in which
fifteen Hurricanes fought for half an hour with between one hundred and
fifty and two hundred German bombers and fighters.' He used up every
last scrap of ammunition and his plane was riddled with bullet holes
when Roald finally landed back at the base. Of the twelve Hurricanes that
had gone into battle that morning, five were shot down and four of their
pilots were killed.

Roald had no idea whether he had killed any enemy soldiers in the
crossfire, although he was later told that out of the twenty-two German
aircraft shot down, at least two kills were probably his: 'It was truly the most
breathless and exhilarating time I have ever had in my life,' he explained
proudly afterwards. 'It was an endless blur of enemy fighters whizzing
towards me from every side.' It was a triumphant moment for the surviving
brave pilots, although they lost their well respected leader Pat Pattle. Before
they had a chance to celebrate their success, the aircraft hangar where their
planes were being repaired was bombed. Several more Hurricanes were
destroyed and the base was all but flattened. The last remaining pilots
wanted to fly back to North Africa where they felt they could be more use to
the war effort, but their commanding officer Air Commodore Grigson had
other plans for Roald, and said he was being entrusted to deliver a valuable
package which needed to be returned to someone waiting back at their
original airbase in Elevsis. Roald knew better than to ask any questions and
simply followed his orders and delivered the package before joining the rest
of his squadron who were waiting at a small airfield in Argos. They were not
safe there either, their white tents were easily visible and within hours that
base had also been attacked by the Luftwaffe; another thirteen Hurricanes
were destroyed.

After just ten days in Greece, Roald was evacuated back to Egypt and made his way straight to the Peels where he spent a month recuperating. But the war was raging on, and he felt he needed to be part of it. He wanted to be serving his country in the only way he knew, so when he heard at the start of May that the remaining members of 80 Squadron were reassembling in Haifa, Roald bought himself a car to drive to Israel where the rest of his original team had been assigned to protecting French airbases. As well as being reunited with some of his old friends, twelve new pilots had been recruited to boost the squadron and together they embarked on another dangerous campaign, during which four of them were killed. Although he was still officially only a pilot officer on probation, Roald was among the pilots who flew sorties over French airbases every day for four weeks, spending long hours in the air and ultimately shooting down two planes. First he hit a Vichy French Air Force Potez 63 on 8 June and then another Ju-88 on 15 June, but his terrible headaches returned. He said it was like having a knife in his forehead; when he started to black out, Roald was suspended from flying and RAF doctors sent him home to Britain.

His record was impressive and he was promoted to War Substantive Flying Officer but after thirty-two active days in the air, Roald's days as a fighter pilot were over and he was devastated at no longer being able to do anything to help bring about a victory. He wrote to his mother: 'It's a pity because I've just got going.' The Second World War continued but Roald joined a convoy of ships sailing around Africa and back to England. He caught a train from the docks at Liverpool down to London, and then a bus back to Buckinghamshire where his mother and sisters had been living since the house in Bexley was bombed.

After three long years away from home, he was eventually reunited with his family. On the journey Roald had written a list of the pilots he knew who had died, and kept it with him for the rest of his life, as a constant reminder of how lucky he had been to survive the war.

Chapter Four

Returning to England in the autumn of 1941 was a peculiar experience for Roald. He had left as a wide-eyed boy in search of adventure, and returned a battle-scarred and broken man. He had killed and almost been killed. After that he found the countryside eerily quiet and struggled to adjust back into ordinary life. His mother had swapped the rambling house in Bexley for a cramped farmhouse in a Buckinghamshire village, Grendon Cottage, and wartime rationing was in full force. His sisters Alfhild and Else were married with young families of their own, and Asta was rarely home either.

Like many soldiers returning from the battlefields, Roald felt out of place and lonely. He befriended some local children whose father, another RAF pilot, had been killed in a crash. Out of a strong sense of loyalty Roald spent hours entertaining them with stories he dreamt up, and found himself much more comfortable in the company of children than adults who asked him difficult questions. He sorely missed the close bond he had forged with his RAF squadron as they risked their lives together on the frontline, and he longed to be in the thick of the action again, but he knew that the only way back into service was to take a desk job, and he could not bear that idea. He wrote: 'To a pilot, being alive but earthbound is worse than not being alive at all.'

Instead he pottered about in his mother's garden and contemplated his future while focusing on recovering his health sufficiently to become a flying instructor. He was posted to an RAF training camp in Uxbridge where he aimed to train new recruits, but it was suggested to Roald that military intelligence was generally considered to be the best option for men in his position. Roald had the right education and social standing, but the shadowy world of espionage was not one he fully understood. He was well connected however, and found himself invited to a dinner in London one evening in March 1942 where he caught the attention of former First World War flying ace Major Harold Balfour, who was by then a Conservative MP working closely with Churchill's War Cabinet as the Under-Secretary of State for Air. Far from being intimidated by meeting a senior officer in such high command, Roald chatted confidently with Balfour and impressed him with his relaxed personality as much as his impressive war record.

Balfour was looking for someone to represent the RAF in the States, to convince doubtful Americans that joining the Allied forces was the right thing to do. The right candidate would need to be charming, have impeccable manners and be an excellent public speaker, and Roald seemed to fit the bill perfectly. Balfour insisted that Roald take up his offer to join the British Embassy in Washington DC as an air attaché immediately.

Roald was reluctant at first, unsure what was expected of him, but Balfour explained that his role would be to help smoothly tie the Americans into the British war effort, which they had only just joined following the Japanese attack on Pearl Harbour the previous December.

Within days Roald found himself boarding the SS *Batori* from Glasgow to Halifax in Canada. From there he took a sleeper train to Montreal and then on to Washington, finally arriving a week later. After enduring months of meagre war rations in England, Roald was astounded by the plentiful food supplies in America, and immediately fell in love with his new surroundings. He sent his mother the first of many large food parcels, and told her about the thrill of travelling first class and staying in luxurious hotels.

Roald liked the atmosphere in Washington, and the house he shared with another attaché in Georgetown, but when he was introduced to dignitaries at the Embassy he found it difficult to put a positive spin on the horrors he had witnessed as a pilot. His job was to glorify battle but he admitted:

> I'd just come from the war. People were getting killed. I had been flying around, seeing horrible things. Now, almost instantly, found myself in the middle of a pre-war cocktail mob in America. I had to dress up in ghastly gold braid and tassels. The result was, I became rather outspoken and brash.

As an air attaché he was there to neutralise the isolationist views still held by many Americans, but when Roald arrived at the British Air Mission, attached to the British embassy, he did not get on particularly well with the ambassador Lord Halifax. He did however strike up what would turn out to be a lifelong friendship with the Texan oil baron Charles Marsh, who was among those Roald had been sent to charm. A popular weekly magazine called *The Saturday Evening Post* sent British novelist C. S. Forester to interview Roald about his flying experiences; Forester was working for the British Ministry of Information, writing propaganda pieces for the American allies. The two men hit it off straight away, and Roald cheerfully offered to write up the flying anecdotes himself that evening, saving Forester the trouble. That was the moment that Roald knew he would be a writer, and later described it as an 'epiphany' because it was the first time he could remember transforming his own experiences and memories into imaginative prose.

Within five hours the story was finished and Roald was hooked. In his book *Lucky Break* he later recalled: 'For the first time in my life, I became totally absorbed in what I was doing.' But he admitted that he was not particularly interested in getting all the facts straight, and showed such a flagrant disregard for the truth that he decided to make the story of his crash far more exciting by claiming he had been shot down by a barrage of enemy fire: 'For me the pleasure of writing comes with inventing stories,' he explained.

That first piece he wrote, which he called *A Piece of Cake*, was more fanciful fiction than factual journalism, and needed to be altered and edited considerably prior to publication, and Roald objected to the new title, *Shot Down Over Libya*, when it eventually appeared in August 1942.

But it landed him his first agent, Harold Matson, who called him 'a natural writer of superior quality'. Roald had made his literary debut and never looked back. From then on he would delight in inventing ever more colourful details to embellish his anecdotes, a gift which of course made him such a great storyteller. He was doing so well in Washington that Roald was soon promoted to Flight Lieutenant War Substantive in 1942 and started to make some highly influential friends. Roald was working alongside other high ranking British officers including Ian Fleming, who would go on to write the James Bond novels, and David Ogilvy, later known as the 'Father of Advertising', who were also both there to help combat the America First anti-war movement. As part of their work the air attaches were introduced to the activities of Canadian spymaster William Stephenson, known by the codename Intrepid. He and Roald became great friends as he passed intelligence about the President Franklin D. Roosevelt to Dahl, which he then dispatched from Washington to the British Prime Minister Winston Churchill. He explained: 'My job was to try and help Winston get on with FDR, and tell Winston what was in the old boy's mind.'

Roald also supplied information back to Stephenson's organisation, the British Security Coordination, which was a part of the British Government department MI6. Roald still suffered from terrible headaches as a result of his head injury, but he settled into life in Washington well. His work mostly involved preparing patriotic speeches about the RAF, which had to be delivered to people who infuriated him with their lack of frontline war experience. He would often have a few drinks before addressing 'po-faced, cod-eyed' audiences. Roald was a confident speaker, but found the audiences tended to enjoy his typically blunt delivery even more if he was slightly drunk. He was so popular that he was soon promoted to the rank of Temporary Wing Commander, in tribute to his five aerial battle victories.

It had not yet occurred to Roald that he could make a living out of fiction, but he enjoyed dabbling with it most evenings, at first making up stories about Gremlins, the imaginary creatures that RAF pilots pretended were responsible for problems in their planes. Roald described them as: 'Little types with horns and a long tail, who walk about on the wings of your aircraft boring holes in the fuselage and urinating in your fuse box.'

He became passionate about his new hobby and would lose himself in writing, welcoming the distraction from the routine of his day job, and his poor health. His first story, *Gremlin Lore*, was basically a fairy tale for children about 'A tribe of funny little people' who lived happily in a forest until huge ugly monsters started chopping down the trees to build airstrips. The Gremlins took their revenge on the 'big tin birds' by causing accidents and making pilots crash their planes. The hero of his story, a British pilot called Gus, crash landed his plane after destructive little Gremlins bored holes in the wings of his Hurricane. But they eventually became friends and the mischievous creature helped the pilot pass his medical examination so that he could return to flying.

Roald typed up the story and sent it off to the British Embassy and the Air Ministry in London, in the hope that they might be able to use it as propaganda material to raise American interest in the RAF. Most of the civil servants who read the manuscript were completely baffled by it and could not understand what Roald hoped to achieve, but Aubrey Morgan who ran the British Information Services in New York was intrigued and showed it to a young movie producer he knew called Sydney Bernstein. Bernstein loved it and immediately sent the story on to his friend Walt Disney.

Disney saw 'great potential' in the Gremlin story and wanted to snap up the film rights straight away. He could instantly picture them as adorable cartoon characters and could predict the lucrative merchandising opportunities. But Roald was very protective of his story and argued relentlessly with Disney's elaborate ideas to develop the story. They suggested numerous other scenarios in which they could send the fictitious Gremlins off on other naughty exploits. Roald hated all their new ideas, and was determined that the Gremlins should only be involved with RAF pilots. Studio bosses sent to meet him in Washington found him stubborn and uncooperative. He still had immense loyalty to his squadron, and felt very strongly that he owed it to them to stick as closely as possible to the tales they had told one another back at the airbases in North Africa and Greece about Gremlins sabotaging their engines.

It was his first taste of the movie business and Roald was not impressed, so he decided to try and sell a shortened version of the story to various different American magazines instead. Brimming with confidence, he boasted to them about his connections to Disney, but took offence when editors suggested making further cuts, or asked him to work alongside more experienced writers. Again Roald stubbornly stood his ground and refused point blank to consider any changes to alter his original work, leaving magazine bosses stunned by the arrogance of such a young writer who had yet to have anything published. Meanwhile, Roald's RAF bosses were annoyed at the amount of time he was spending negotiating publishing rights when he should have been doing his job, and so his agent Harold Matson stepped in to handle the deals on his behalf. He could see the sound business sense in striking up a profitable working partnership with Disney and managed to get a new offer on the table, this time proposing that a chunk of the profits be donated to the RAF Benevolent Fund. But Roald was tired of being fobbed off by money men, and resented having to wrangle with Disney's copyright lawyer Frank Waldheim who he described as 'a dark cunning little Jew', an early sign of the anti-Semitic views which would come to tarnish Roald's reputation in years to come.

He wanted to sit down and thrash out the details with Walt Disney himself. Roald may have been new to the entertainment industry but he certainly was not lacking in self-belief, and was determined to have his say over pretty much every single aspect of the film production. Disney was less concerned about plotline and more worried about various copyright issues which he feared may rear up since Roald had not actually invented the Gremlin characters himself. They were a well known part of RAF folklore, but since nobody came forward to claim to know how the legend had originally started many years earlier, Roald could claim ownership and agreed to sign a contract that suited all sides. He agreed that Disney's illustrators would provide the images for the story, which would first be published across seven pages in *Cosmopolitan* magazine, but of course Roald had very specific ideas about the illustrations and had a crystal clear vision in his head of exactly what the Gremlins should look like.

He felt very strongly that it was his duty to all RAF pilots, past and present, to portray the mythical characters accurately, and gave copious notes to the illustrators down to the smallest detail – even insisting they wore little green bowler hats when they were not flying.

But when he saw the initial drawings, Roald complained furiously:

> There should be a great deal more expression on the face, which actually has an almost human appearance. The Leprechorn or Woffledigit, as I intend to call it, has been represented as an old gnome-like man with six legs, whereas I explain very carefully in the story that he looks like a wolf. I really do know what they look like, having seen a great number of them in my time.

In the hope of speeding up the project, Disney sent a personal invitation for Roald to fly out to visit the studios in California, adding that he would put him up in the exclusive Beverly Hills Hotel for two weeks as his guest. Disney assigned six artists to work closely with Roald during his trip to perfect the illustrations for a children's picture book that would accompany the film when it was eventually released.

Roald agreed to fly to Los Angeles but his host's generosity did nothing to butter him up and when he arrived he remained as adamant as ever about the precise look of each character, and continued to fight his corner. The film was expected to be a mixture of live action RAF footage interspersed with Disney cartoons, but Roald was shocked to find that Walt Disney did not do much of the drawing himself, and had an explosive temper. Roald described him as 'quite an erk' – RAF slang for non-flying ground staff, but Disney liked Roald and they formed an unlikely friendship, with the Mickey Mouse creator giving him the affectionate nickname of 'Stalky' because he was so tall.

He loved Los Angeles however, and was thrilled when the studio threw a glitzy party in his honour, with celebrities acting out the roles of different Gremlins. Even Charlie Chaplin pretended to be one of his creations, a Widget. The same night he met the glamorous actress Phyllis Brooks, who had previously dated Cary Grant and Howard Hughes, and was immediately besotted with her. They spent the rest of his trip together but the fling ended as quickly as it began, and just six months later he admitted: 'She wants to shoot me.' Young and dashing, Roald tended to turn up to events sharply dressed in his formal RAF uniform and quickly gained a reputation as something of a ladies man.

After Roald's visit to the studio, having made his vision clear, plans for the film began to develop much more rapidly. Disney abandoned the idea of using live action footage, and decided it should be all animation, experimenting with various new storylines which all involved Gremlins helping the RAF defeat the Nazis at some point. By the time Roald received the finished script, word had spread to London where publishers were clamouring to get their hands on the UK rights to the story, comedians were cracking jokes about Gremlins being to blame for all kinds of disasters, and mainstream magazines including *Time* and *Newsweek* were running pieces about the phenomenon, all of which served to boost the hype around the forthcoming film even further.

Roald had inadvertently become a celebrity and was thoroughly enjoying his new found taste of fame. He felt he had done the RAF a great service by negotiating such lucrative terms for them and, having agreed to donate most of his royalties to Air Force charities, he simply could not understand why some of his senior bosses thought he was getting too big for his boots.

Philosopher Isiah Berlin, who was then working for the British Diplomatic Service, described him as 'Extremely conceited, and entitled to respect and very special treatment.' Although Roald had written the book in his own spare time and used his allocated days of annual leave to visit the Disney studios, he was warned by the top brass to tread a little more carefully when he announced he would need to spend more time in Hollywood developing the project further. Roald was feeling undervalued by the RAF and got the distinct impression that the military was trying to distance itself from what was clearly being seen as a frivolous Disney project; he was insulted that they appeared to be treating his Gremlins as something of a joke. Roald insisted repeatedly that it was not for his own benefit, and all he wanted was to make money for needy airmen and bereaved families. When it was suggested that the RAF take full control of the profits and pay him a cut, he was even more upset at not getting the recognition he had hoped for. Eventually he negotiated a deal that allowed him to keep twenty per cent of the profits for his own charitable fund which would help the mothers of pilots from his former squadron who had been killed in action. At several stages along the line Roald considered pulling the plug on the entire project, but the book *The Gremlins* was already in production, and once it was published in April 1943 it seemed there was no turning back. The book was emblazoned with the words 'From the Walt Disney Production', and the cover showed three naughty Gremlins wrecking a fighter plane.

The book flew off the shelves, and the initial print run of 50,000 copies sold out immediately – even the First Lady Eleanor Roosevelt said she found the story 'delightful'. Plans to reprint a further 25,000 copies were only abandoned because of restrictions forced on the publisher by wartime paper shortages. Toys of the characters Fifinella and Widget were hugely popular too, but behind the scenes Roald was still picking apart the film script and felt that the cartoon illustrations lacked the humanity which animals had in other recent Disney movies such as *Bambi* and *Dumbo*.

Disney begged his friend Stalky to fly back out to California so they could sit down and work on the script together but Roald was already slightly bored with the whole idea, and knew the RAF would be reluctant to give him yet more time off. In the end, at Disney's insistence, he agreed to take ten days unpaid leave in the hope of wrapping the project up for good, concerned that the war could be over before the film was finished. When he arrived at Disney's office, Roald insisted they spend twelve hours a day finalising the script, but at some point in the trip Roald still managed to find the time to take the actress Ginger Rogers out for dinner.

Progress was painfully slow however, and in December 1943 when it seemed they had hardly inched any further forward, Disney finally took the decision to abandon the film entirely, telling Roald that they were pulling the plug but that he could buy back the rights for $20,000. At the time that was an amount he could not possibly afford, and he walked away with nothing – although the characters reappeared in his first novel two years later. Roald's Hollywood adventure appeared to be over, he felt deeply disappointed and blamed Walt Disney for failing to understand the English essence of the Gremlins. 'It could have been successful,' he told a Disney historian years later. 'He had no feeling for England in any way. He was a hundred per cent American.'

He retreated to Washington to lick his wounds, and consoled himself by splashing out on a new set of false teeth, taking the radical step of having all his real teeth removed as a painful precautionary measure against future bouts of toothache and expensive dental treatments. He was so adamant that it was a sensible move that he even convinced his mother to follow suit, and she too had her teeth extracted at the Harley Street dentist he recommended.

Roald struggled to settle back into his old routine. Although he was charming and popular, Roald was not naturally sociable or diplomatic and refused most of the invitations he received, preferring to spend his evenings alone at home writing and drinking. He had to force himself to play the part of the smooth English airman and struggled to make friends, until he unexpectedly came to the attention of the liberal Vice President Henry Wallace, who had a keen interest in film making and wanted to hear all about his experiences with Disney.

Roald had been introduced to him by a young producer called Gabriel Pascal, a handsome young actor from Transylvania who rose to fame after accidentally blundering on to a film set in Hungary, while riding a horse naked! After Pascal read *Introducing The Gremlins* he was keen to work with Roald on a new idea he had for a film about Henry Wallace. Roald also struck up an unlikely friendship with playwright George Bernard Shaw, and after the pair got talking on a nudist beach in the south of France, Shaw sold him the film rights to his plays *Pygmalion* and *Major Barbara*.

Suddenly Roald was mixing with the most influential politicians in the world, and was immensely flattered to be considered a part of their high-powered circles. He wrote to his mother:

> I found myself having lunch with the Vice Pres of the United States and talking to him from one o'clock until 6 p.m. He said he wanted me to give up my job for three months, retire into the mountains somewhere and write the script! I said no, I wouldn't – but if he liked I would try and do it in my spare time.

Wallace himself asked Lord Halifax to give Roald time off from the Embassy so that they could develop his project together, and soon they were meeting every day to discuss ideas for a film script. Roald was even introduced to President Roosevelt himself who was also taking a keen personal interest in the film, which would be based on the Vice President's inspirational philosophy of how to tackle the problems facing people in post-war America.

One of the main locations was to be the Virginia estate of Charles Marsh, the wealthy Texan who had originally introduced Gabriel Pascal to Henry Wallace. Although Marsh was thirty years older than Roald, they had met before and struck up a close friendship from the start. Charles became a highly influential father figure to Roald for many years. He loved to hear all the latest political gossip from the British Embassy and relied on Roald to share with him how Roosevelt was feeling about various key matters of the day. The two men also shared a passion for storytelling, and Roald delighted in passing on scurrilous pieces of information about their mutual friends.

When the pair had first met in 1943, Charles was married to his second wife Alice, whom he had got pregnant while still with his first wife; Roald had helped him concoct an elaborate story to tell her disapproving parents. Charles arranged for Alice to go on holiday to England, and claimed that while she was away she had had fallen in love with a soldier who had been killed by bandits, leaving her pregnant. By this time, Charles was divorced and free to marry her and claim the child as his own. The whole episode was fabricated in order to make his own daughter appear legitimate. But Roald loved this eccentric side of his new mentor. Roald was soon part of the family, and later described Charles as his 'best friend in the world'.

Chapter Five

Gradually Roald was building a reputation as a writer and offers of work were starting to come his way, although not enough for him to give up the day job quite yet. He was invited to write the screenplay for Paul Gallico's novel *The Snow Goose* and the film director Howard Hawks asked to work with him too; even though both film projects were eventually shelved, Roald spent every evening at his writing desk, usually with a bottle of brandy at his side.

Any spare time he had was spent writing fiction, and most of the stories he came up with at the time were written in the first person and centred around pilots and their mothers, as well as the risks associated with wartime flying. Roald was still haunted by his plane crash and sharply aware that he had cheated death, and he revisited these same themes over and over again.

The first of these stories was called *Only This*, about a lonely mother waiting anxiously for her only son, a bomber pilot, to come home. *Katina* told of a Greek girl whose parents were killed by German bombs, and after she was left orphaned was adopted by an RAF squadron. Another short story, *The Ginger Cat*, was about a German bomber landing unexpectedly at an RAF airfield with a cat in the cockpit. The mix of fantasy and reality made each of the stories hugely popular as pieces of propaganda, but Roald was reluctant to take payment for them in case his bosses tried to stop him writing on the side, and instead donated any money he made to his favourite charity – the RAF Benevolent Fund which benefited war widows. Roald also found time to come up with a new short story about a houseboy in Tanganyika, which was immediately published, to great acclaim, by *Atlantic Monthly*.

Major publishing houses began contacting Roald asking what else he had, they were offering to print any longer stories even before he had a chance to write them. Roald was starting to realise that perhaps he would be able to make a full time career out of writing alone, and started to look for a new agent. He felt that Harold Matson had not been looking after his interests as well as he might have liked, and eventually signed with a famous New York based agent called Ann Watkins, a feisty woman who already represented several of Roald's literary heroes including Dylan Thomas and Ernest Hemingway. He and Ann became lifelong friends and he stayed with her agency for over thirty years, even after she retired and handed Roald's affairs over to her son Mike.

Faced with this new and unexpected demand for more fiction, Roald was constantly hunting around for inspiration. He realised he would have to come up with a wider range of subject matter than merely Gremlins and fighter pilots, but he was easily distracted. It did not help that he felt sure his new apartment was haunted. When the owners of the house he had been renting in Washington announced they would be returning home in 1943, Roald needed to find new accommodation in a hurry and ended up renting an apartment where the previous tenant had shot his girlfriend in a jealous fight over her secret lover. There was still blood on the walls and bullet holes in the ceiling when Roald moved in, and he admitted to his mother in one of his letters that he did not feel comfortable spending his evenings alone there. He moved out as quickly as he had moved in, and tried sharing a place with one of his colleagues from the British Embassy, but found he was too easily distracted with somebody else in the house. If he was going to spend all of his spare time writing, Roald realised, he would need to live alone.

Some of his colleagues at the Embassy could not understand why his bosses were being quite so lenient with Roald, allowing him extra time off for his various scriptwriting projects, and it has since been suggested that he was being groomed to join a clandestine spying team. The British Security Coordination (BSC), which had initially been established to promote British interests in America, was later involved in training spies. The theory may also explain why Roald was being introduced to the very highest echelons of American political society so early on in his career – he was invited to the White House on various occasions, mingling with the cream of Washington's political elite, although he was often privately highly critical of the people he met.

Over the summer of 1943 he was invited to spend a weekend with the Roosevelts at their country retreat, Hyde Park, to discuss aviation policy. He appeared to be on very friendly terms with the President and First Lady but on his return from the jaunt Roald was expected to supply the Embassy with a detailed ten-page report about various aspects of the estate as well as sharp observations about the inner workings of the President's mind. He and Roosevelt had apparently discussed the President's chances of winning a fourth term in office and even shared their opinions of Prime Minister Winston Churchill. It must have occurred to Roosevelt that there was a high chance everything he said would be reported back by Roald to his bosses, and yet he could often be wildly indiscreet, and occasionally even quite gossipy.

As a result of this powerful new friendship he had struck up, Roald had become a very valuable commodity and was promoted to Squadron Leader, although some in the upper echelons of the RAF were not in favour of such a rapid rise through the ranks, and felt that Roald needed to be brought to heel. One senior figure, Air Marshall William Welsh, flew to Washington from Whitehall in order to object about how outspoken Roald had been. He warned that Roald was in need of 'serious military discipline', and recommended that he be transferred back to London. In October that year, Roald told his mother he had been 'kicked out' and was heading back home, but the RAF needed him and within weeks he was called back to Washington again, having been made fully aware that a dim view was being taken about the openly frank remarks he was known for making, and it could land him in trouble if he did not start to be more discreet. Roald admitted that he was, 'A tactless sort of fellow and that's the one thing a diplomat mustn't be.'

But he was given a major vote of confidence in April 1944 when he was instructed to return to London to report on the political situation in America for one of his literary heroes, Ernest Hemingway, before he was sent to report on the D-Day landings at Normandy for the RAF. The next time he returned to Washington, in July, he was officially employed by the BSC and was promoted once again to Wing Commander. The RAF bosses who had wanted to be rid of Roald were probably not happy to see him back in an even more powerful position, but there was nothing they could do, he had established himself as a very useful asset. Fortunately for all concerned he was soon relocated to New York, in the hope he could charm Manhattan society in an equally successful way. Roald never forgot the first time he arrived at the BSC's slick offices in Rockefeller Centre, where he was particularly impressed with the fast moving glass elevators which of course would feature so prominently in Willy Wonka's magical empire, in both *Charlie and The Chocolate Factory* and *Charlie and the Great Glass Elevator*. Roald wrote home, effusively exclaiming: 'Your ears pop and your stomach either comes out of your mouth or drops out of your arse according to whether you are going up or down.'

It was immediately apparent to Roald's new colleagues that he was there because of his impressive talent for befriending the great and the good. Somehow he never appeared star struck or intimidated by high-ranking politicians or any of the most powerful members of Manhattan society who all felt relaxed enough around him to share sensitive information, and sometimes even their most intimate secrets – simply because he asked. 'I was able to ask pointed questions and get equally pointed replies because, theoretically, I was a nobody,' he recalled.

He was being paid to keep his ear to the ground, while pushing British interests in whichever direction was deemed appropriate. Roald soon became something of an expert when it came to flirting and charming information out of women too. He found that the wives of powerful men often felt neglected by their busy husbands and could be persuaded to let all kind of valuable titbits slip if they were given enough of the right kind of attention.

Great losses in the war had left a significant shortage of eligible young men in New York, and since the reason he was there was to attend as many cocktail parties, dinners, book launches and charity functions as possible, invitations were soon pouring in.

He discovered that wealthy, sophisticated – and often married – women tended to be attracted to him, and he usually had several admirers fluttering around him at any one time. The editor of *Ladies Home Journal* Beatrice Gould admitted she was drawn to his 'manly beauty', and published many of his early stories in her magazine. Needless to say it helped that First Lady Eleanor Roosevelt sang his praises, his connection to the President opened many doors, although according to Charles Marsh's daughter, Antoinette Haskell, it was because he was 'drop dead gorgeous'. Antoinette added: 'He was very arrogant with his women, but he got away with it. The uniform didn't hurt one bit – and he was an ace. I think he slept with everybody on the east and west coasts that had more than fifty thousand dollars a year.'

One of the many women who fell prey to Roald's charms was a glamorous widow called Evalyn Walsh McLean who he described as 'fantastic and rather stupid'. Evalyn invited him to dozens of parties and flirted with him almost constantly, to his great amusement. Roald wrote to his mother: 'I can't help looking down and seeing the closely guarded secret of her finely shaped bosoms. She has enormous pads stuffed into her shirt front, and the effect is very good to anyone who is under 6' 5" in height.'

CHAPTER FIVE

She was just one of many society hostesses who was delighted whenever Roald accepted an invitation since she relished the way he tended to stir up controversial debates over otherwise dull dinners, making them the most gossiped about events. Roald thrived in these environments and enthusiastically accepted any chance to make mischief that came his way.

He was also a regular guest of Helen Rogers Reid, the 60-year-old wife of media magnate Ogden Mills Reid, the owner of the *New York Tribune* and the *New York Herald Tribune*. She had great influence over the editorial stance of her husband's newspapers, and since she was a prominent anglophile and adored Roald, she was an influential friend for him to make.

Helen thoroughly enjoyed matchmaking for Roald and introduced him to a number of attractive women whom he cheerfully took out on the town, but was reluctant to commit to any of them emotionally and was becoming something of a cad. Helen set him up with actress Nancy Carroll, who was divorced and much older than him at 39, but while they were out on a date, at the premiere of a propaganda movie called *Eagle Squadron*, Roald was distracted by another useful female contact, Congresswoman Clare Booth Luce, whose husband owned *Time* and *Life* magazines. Although he had arrived at the premiere with Nancy, he left that evening with Mrs Luce, who was thirteen years his senior, and did not return home until the following day. Roald even bragged about his shameless conquest to his mother: 'I got home to the house of my host at 9 a.m. the next morning. And failed to make my room without being seen to ruffle the bedclothes. I had to do a lot of talking to re-establish my reputation.'

Roald considered it not only his job, but also his patriotic duty, to encourage these publications to take a more pro-British stance, and he rose to the challenge with relish for months. But eventually he tired of the 'assignment', and one morning announced to his boss that he was 'all fucked out' because Mrs Luce 'had screwed him from one end of the room to the other for three goddamn nights'. Regardless of whether this particular tale of Roald's womanising ways was true or not – and many were convinced it was not – he found the frequent retelling of it highly amusing.

He was also rumoured to have had affairs with numerous other wealthy, older, married women including Barbara Hutton, English actress Leonora Corbett, who had also been linked to *Winnie the Pooh* author A. A. Milne, and the writer Martha Gellhorn, who said she found him 'very, very attractive and slightly mad.' His most significant conquest that year (1944) was the 41-year-old oil heiress Millicent Rogers who impressed him with her excellent social connections and the impressive art collections she had displayed on the walls of her various properties around the country. Millicent seemed besotted with Roald and gave him a key to her front door. But while he made full use of her luxurious home whenever he got the chance, he made fun of her behind her back, and gave her the unflattering nickname 'Curvature' as a result of her slight stoop.

Although Millicent enjoyed showering her lover with expensive gifts, she was also rumoured to be having another affair at the same time with his colleague Ian Fleming – and Roald soon tired of her, her friends and what he saw as their rather decadent lifestyles. Describing a visit to one of her houses, Roald wrote:

> Women with ruby necklaces and sapphire necklaces and God knows what else sauntered in and out and down below amidst miles of corridors. There were swimming baths, Turkish baths, colonic lavages, heat treatment rooms and everything else which is calculated to make the prematurely aging playboys and playwomen age a little less quickly. I didn't like it much.

Roald was not looking for a girlfriend, he insisted that he was only interested in desire, not love, and that relationships were based on seventy per cent sexual attraction and only thirty per cent on mutual respect anyway. As a result of this firmly held belief, most of Roald's short-lived affairs tended to end badly. His friend David Ogilvy explained: 'When they fell in love with him, as a lot did, I don't think he was nice to them.'

There was, finally, one woman who managed to keep Roald's attention a little longer than the rest, a French actress called Susanne Charpentier, known as Annabella. Although she was married to her third husband, American actor Tyrone Power, the unconventional couple had an open marriage and were free to pursue other relationships. When Annabella met Roald at a party, she made it quite clear that her husband would not mind since he was already seeing actress Judy Garland. Roald told his mother afterwards: 'She's an intelligent dame and much fun.' They ended up seeing each other on and off for most of 1944, and Annabella recalled: 'It was like we were twin brothers. Romantic? Not really. Physical? Sometimes. But most important we had a complete understanding and he trusted me.' Years later she recalled that they behaved 'like naughty schoolboys together'.

While his love life may have been giving him great pleasure, at the age of just 28 Roald was already limping like an old man as various doctors and osteopaths had been unable to help ease the agony of the spinal injury which had plagued him since the plane crash in Libya. He was miserable from having to endure almost constant pain and even though there were times when he was so uncomfortable that he could barely find a way to read or write, he tried to live with it as best he could because he dreaded the idea of having to undergo major surgery.

Towards the end of the year he was invited to an exclusive private dinner party to celebrate President Roosevelt being re-elected, but other guests noticed that he was clearly in some discomfort and barely able to eat anything. Charles Marsh invited him to spend Christmas with his family at their estate in Virginia where it became impossible for Roald to hide his back problems. He was drinking so heavily in a bid to numb the pain that Charles was worried, and urged him to have the surgery, insisting he would pay for all the medical bills if that was part of the reason for his reluctance.

Roald needed to have a disc removed and had to spend the following four weeks in bed while he recuperated. Two further procedures were required after that and then he was struck down by a bout of severe appendicitis, meaning he was in and out of hospital for months. Charles paid for everything as promised, and invited Roald to convalesce in the lap of luxury at his mansion in Palm Springs, California. The warmth did him good but by the time Roald was declared fit enough to return to work back in New York, President Roosevelt was dead and he began to feel that this chapter in his life was coming to a close. He was suspicious of the new political regime, increasingly homesick and desperate to concentrate on writing. He had landed a contract to publish *Over To You*, his collection of short stories, and his sister Else was pregnant, so Roald prepared to fly home for good that summer.

His plans were scuppered by the Canadian millionaire businessman William Stephenson, who managed to persuade Roald to stay on for just a few more months. Stephenson wanted Roald to write a history of the British Security Coordination to help clear up the many misconceptions about the organisation. People had long been intrigued by the shadowy secret service network and there were numerous rumours about the exact nature of the complex, clandestine undercover operations which were being run from the Rockefeller Centre in the heart of New York. Officially the BSC was only promoting British interests in the States, but at the same time they were also training spies, and Stephenson was thought to be coordinating a far-reaching network of more than a thousand secret agents.

Roald agreed, although his heart was not in it, and his spirits sank even lower when he was sent to a remote military base at Lake Ontario in Canada, known only as Camp X, to learn more about the BSC's covert operations. Recruits had been sent there in the past to learn sabotage techniques, code breaking and how to interrogate prisoners. It was where Ian Fleming learned many of the spying tricks and techniques he would later use in his famous James Bond stories. By the time Roald arrived, Camp X was little more than a storage space for highly sensitive archive material and he was soon bored by the task in hand. He felt isolated and found the atmosphere of secrecy immensely irritating. The living conditions were basic, and a far cry from the luxurious lifestyle he had got accustomed to thanks to the wealthy friends he had made in New York, Washington and California. Worse still, strict liquor licensing laws meant he could only buy one bottle of spirits a month.

He played golf and took long walks around the lake to avoid starting work on the book, which was intended to glamorise the American defeat of Nazi Germany, but Roald was unsettled when he started his research and learned about some of the unit's more sinister tactics being deployed to 'toughen up' the returning troops in anticipation of another attack by the Germans.

Shortly after his arrival, the bombing of Hiroshima and Nagasaki in Japan by the US signalled that the Second World War was officially over and he could be released from his military duties. Roald was already longing for a fresh challenge when he left Camp X in September 1945 and returned home at last.

Chapter Six

After a brief spell saying his goodbyes in New York, Roald set sail for home in February 1946, having spent most of the past eight years abroad. It had been a turbulent time but Roald knew he had been one of the lucky ones. So many young men had not survived the conflict, but he had made the best of the opportunities that had come his way, and gathered some useful contacts. He may have broken more than his fair share of hearts, but Roald was now friends with powerful politicians, glamorous film stars and wealthy businessmen.

He arrived home a changed man; suave and sophisticated, he no longer craved adventure and excitement, he had a far more cynical outlook on the world. The death and devastation he had witnessed during the war weighed heavily on his shoulders, and the atomic bombings made him fearful about the future. As his ship docked on British shores, Roald was saddened by what he saw. His once proud country now seemed desolate, with its people disillusioned, distressed and grieving. Many cities had been ravaged by bombs and Britain teetered on the brink of economic collapse. There was much to celebrate once peace had been declared, but when American political support was withdrawn the future looked increasingly uncertain. Fuel shortages plunged much of the country into darkness, food became scarce again, unemployment soared and crime was rife.

There was not yet any sign of the social reform which had been promised in the aftermath of Winston Churchill's defeat in 1945, and although Roald himself supported the new government he was worried that the peace would not last. Shocked and utterly depressed by the devastation he saw in London, Roald decided he would be happier living in the countryside, where his great love of nature inspired him. His experiences had matured him, and now the only thing he really wanted was to see if he could make it as a writer. In his short story *Someone Like You* he described the effect of war on a young fighter pilot, a man who seemed not unlike Roald himself:

> From being a bouncing boy he had become someone old and
> wise and gentle ... like a tired man of seventy years. He had

41

become so different and he had changed so much that at first
it was embarrassing and it was not easy to know what to say.

Roald was drawing a small monthly invalid pension from the RAF and he
had the inheritance his father had left him in a trust fund, but he assured his
mother they could grow all the extra food they needed in her large garden.
Roald was relieved to have a complete break from the world of political
intrigue. He had enjoyed his taste of the fast-paced glitz of Hollywood too,
but felt ready to surround himself instead with nature and animals. He
bought six dogs, including a racing greyhound and a dachshund, ducks,
a parrot and a canary in a bid to lift his spirits as *Over To You* was not
proving the success he had hoped for. The reviews were mixed, and Roald
decided to concentrate instead on writing a more serious novel focusing
on the fears he shared with so many people about the destruction caused
by atomic bombs.

He was terrified for the future of humanity, and now when he wrote
about his beloved Gremlin characters they had been transformed from
impish little troublemakers into more sinister, evil trolls. He described
them as: 'Weird and frightening with a deathless, ageless expression in
the small black lidless eyes, with a cunning twist about the small, thick-
lipped mouth.' The female Gremlins, who Walt Disney had visualised
as wide-eyed flirts, became grotesque, and he wrote that they were:
'Bald-headed and ugly as hell, worse, far worse than the male because
the female of any type is always more scheming, cunning, jealous and
relentless than the male.'

In his latest story, the destruction wrought by the atomic bomb had driven
the Gremlins underground. Roald wrote: 'Deep down below the ground the
Gremlins heard the distant whoof and roar of huge explosions; they felt the
earth tremble. Impatiently they waited to see how great the destruction had
been and whether the killing was complete.'

As the post-war political situation continued to look uncertain, Roald
was unsettled. He obsessed about the possibility of a nuclear holocaust,
and frequently wrote to Charles Marsh about the outbreak of a third world
war which he feared was inevitable: 'I'm frightened of war,' he wrote. 'Not
just frightened of it. Just appalled by it and its coming. It's the saddest and
craziest thought that it's possible to think.'

Roald deliberately kept away from political debates among his friends in
London, preferring the tranquil seclusion of his mother's rural farmhouse,
but he remained deeply pessimistic about the outside world, convinced that

a further global conflict was imminent. He felt sure it was not a case of if, but simply when, the country would be at war again. In another of his regular letters to Charles he wrote:

> Oh dear the world is really a thick thing. There always has been war before in the world and I suppose there always will be. To try and stop one nation among many from misbehaving periodically is just as difficult as trying to stop crime in a country.

He soon finished his novel and called it *Some Time Never*. He intended for it to be a satire of the global issues that worried him, particularly the fear and apprehension felt by fighter pilots on the frontlines. Much of the story is bleak and disturbing to read, the main character, Peternip, is constantly engulfed by a sense of dark despair: 'Nothing counted … that was the simple truth; for the sum total of all things, of living, loving, hating, dying, adds up, when the sum is carefully done to nothing, to precisely nothing,' Peternip thought.

Roald wrote how this character 'despised all human beings, himself included,' and later in the story, when he is robbed of his chance to fly, Peternip plunges into a deep depression. After the protagonist is killed by a bomb in London, the novel turns into a dark look at the destruction of humanity from the point of view of the Gremlins who have lost their leader.

In the end Roald damned the whole of mankind as 'A mountain of conceit and selfishness … a creature who possesses greed and avarice and a love of power.' The book finishes with humanity being entirely destroyed by an atomic apocalypse, and the planet left devastated.

Years later Roald's daughter Ophelia confirmed that the book revealed many of her father's deepest fears: 'He was always very unconflicted about the fact that he felt human beings were capable of really monstrous things,' she said. 'I think he was trying to say something about the futility of war.'

Finishing the book so fast left Roald both physically and mentally exhausted. He had only been back in Britain for a month but his obsession with completing *Some Time Never* had consumed him. He hired his sister Asta as his typist but she told him the story 'didn't work' and he started to lose his confidence. He felt lonely and realised he was lacking the friends and confidantes he had in America who had always championed his writing and showered him with praise.

He moved into a cottage in the grounds of his mother's new farm but tended to keep to himself and rarely confided in his family. He thought he might lift his spirits by trying to meet some women, but there did not seem to be many suitable prospects in the village. His sister Alfhild recalled him going up to London to meet 'call girls', and that for a time he was dating both the actress Ann Darcy and a war widow to whom he gave an expensive bracelet that Millicent Rogers had given him in New York.

Sex was always important to Roald, even if emotional intimacy was not, and in his next novel *Fifty Thousand Frogskins* he dared to write about it for the first time. His main character, Gordon Hawes, was a callous lothario, while his sidekick Sidney Cubbage was sex-starved and desperate. Hawes, who kept body hair which he surreptitiously snipped from each of his many conquests as a gruesome souvenir, told Cubbage: 'There's nothing respectable about women. Every woman is a whore at heart.' He also argued that sex itself was: 'Messy, slightly acrobatic and very undignified. It is indecent, even between a bishop and his wife. You try doing it with your wife in a public park. You'll soon find out whether it is indecent or not.'

He may have had a high sex drive, but Roald was hindered in his pursuits by his back pain which was becoming worse than ever, and he ended up spending Christmas 1946 stuck in the Military Hospital for Head Injuries because he was struggling to walk, and his doctors wanted to operate on his spine again. He hated the cold and gloomy hospital where post-war coal shortages meant the boilers were hardly functioning and the ward was freezing cold. He wrote to his agent Ann Watkins:

> Of all the godforsaken places in which to be, this is it. The room is as cold as the tip of an Eskimo's tool. I am flat on the back and floating on a haze of morphine and faraway pain. I do not give a bugger what they do so long as I can sit up in my right senses and get on with some work.

Once he was discharged from the hospital, in January 1947, there was further misery waiting for him as Ann broke the unwelcome news that both *Over To You* and *Some Time Never* were doing rather poorly in America. Sales were disappointingly low and he decided to distance himself from them both and start something new. Roald had become convinced that *Some Time Never* was 'a bad book', and found it difficult to hide his disappointment about the largely scathing review. He told Ann: 'No one I've given it to so far likes it. Depressed about this writing business.'

Roald wanted to base himself in England but struggled to find a decent agent to represent him as he battled to launch his writing career on home soil. In Washington and New York he had moved in high brow literary circles where he played the part of the smooth and handsome outsider with ease, charming everyone he met with his clipped British accent and his immaculate military uniform. Roald had struck up friendships with the likes of Noel Coward and Ernest Hemingway – he even dined with the President and his wife – but in London he struggled to find an agent who believed in his talents. He dismissed the first candidate David Higham as 'a dirty old bastard' and decided the next one he considered, Peter Watt, was 'as much use as a group of matrons at a tea party'. He complained that the situation was so dire and uninspiring that he would even need to have paper and pencils sent over from America if he was to have any success because the limited selection of stationery supplies he was forced to choose from was 'like writing with a piece of charcoal on a lump of gravel'. Roald felt lost, with an overwhelming sense that he did not really belong at home. While he had been away most of his peers had been to university, found regular jobs and started families. Meanwhile he had not felt the need to further his education, had very few friends and felt like he did not have any natural affinity to any particular social or economic class and did not feel drawn to any political party either.

He was living modestly in a remote country cottage in the grounds of his mother's farm, and cut off from literary contacts he had left himself vulnerable to criticism, and had plenty of time to dwell on it. He knew he should probably settle down and find himself a proper job and a wife, but all he really wanted to do was listen to music, and spent hours on end playing gramophone records of his favourite symphonies, and became so knowledgeable on the subject of classical composers that he had the idea of writing solely about music, and thought perhaps he might dabble in journalism. As time wore on Roald realised he was missing some of the little luxuries he had enjoyed in America, fine wine in particular, but was in need of money if he was going to be able to afford the sort of restaurants and clubs he enjoyed. To earn some extra cash he experimented with some gothic short stories, anxious to find a new voice and writing style, and sent them off to newspapers and magazines. But editors found them too disturbing for their readers and even his friends encouraged Roald to lighten up. Feeling even more melancholy, he started to drink heavily and clashed with his mother frequently, she was also drinking a great deal and without any real comprehension of what her son had endured during the war, she could not fathom why he was not married or even earning a regular income. While she was relieved to have Roald home (so many of her friends sons had not returned from battle), Sofie often escaped to a rented cottage in Cornwall to give them both some space and the solitude she craved.

Roald wrote about this strained relationship with his mother in a short story called *People Nowadays*, which he later renamed *The Soldier*, in which a war veteran is trapped in a cold marriage with an unfeeling wife who does not understand what he has been through. The couple live on a farm where the soldier is haunted by nightmares which he tries to counter with memories of his happy childhood holidays. But the wife is unsympathetic and he describes her as an 'awful, cruel bitch' who was occasionally violent towards him.

By the start of 1948 Roald was desperate for a change of scene and when his old friend Charles Marsh offered to fly him out to Jamaica for a month he did not hesitate to accept. He stayed with Ernest Hemingway and swam on Max Beaverbrook's private beach before meeting up with Charles. The holiday was just what Roald needed, and cheered him up enormously. He was great company in Jamaica but his mood did not last for long after his plane touched down in London. He had enjoyed the taste of luxury and returned home even more desperate to start making some decent money. Roald knew he was too old to be living with his mother, and worked around the clock churning out one story after another: 'I shall continue to write and I truly believe that one day I shall produce a really first class novel. The stories I'm doing now may not sell, but they are wonderful practice and I learn a little more with each one I do,' he said.

Roald found it hard to remain optimistic when he was struggling to sell his stories. He tried all kinds of different genres, and even attempted his first, and what he hoped would be his last, romantic love story, but told Ann Watkins it was 'frightful bullshit,' and was sure he had run out of time.

Roald decided he should take a job as a stockbroker in the hope of perhaps making enough money to retire early, and have a chance to write in his old age. But just as he was about to give up all hope, his fortunes suddenly changed. The publishing world finally sat up and began to take notice of Roald Dahl.

Chapter Seven

Down on his luck, Roald was ready to resign himself to returning to the dull and repetitive drudgery of commuting into the city, when quite unexpectedly *Colliers* magazine bought a rather strange story he had submitted about a man who bets with visitors to win the little fingers from their hands, and builds up a gristly collection of bloodied digits.

Roald himself had not thought much about *The Smoker* when he first wrote it, but it would end up becoming one of his most famous stories after legendary film maker Alfred Hitchcock read the magazine and offered Roald a lucrative deal for the television rights to several stories. Hitchcock filmed *The Smoker*, also known as *The Man from the South*, twice as episodes of his series *Alfred Hitchcock Presents* in 1960 and 1985. It became the first story in Roald's original *Tales of the Unexpected* collection and decades later Hollywood director Quentin Tarantino would also adapt the story for a film.

Roald was astounded that his work could be so valuable, and with his first decent pay cheque he celebrated by treating himself to a trip to Paris. When he returned there was another massive confidence boost in store – the magazine sent him a further bonus of $1,000 because the story had been judged the best of the year, and they offered him a further $2,500 to write a love story. He had no interest in romantic fiction but was certainly in no position to turn down that kind of money, and wrote to Ann Watkins:

> All whores have their price. It made me vomit to do it, and
> you know as I do, once a whore, always a whore. But send it
> to them quick and tell them they can cut this one just as much
> as they like. And get that dough.

Soon Roald could afford for him and his mother to move to Wisteria Cottage, a Georgian townhouse in the nearby town of Old Amersham, just a few miles from where they had been living on the farm, but more convenient for Sofie who was increasingly arthritic and wanted to be less isolated. And she threw herself into the new community, quickly gaining a somewhat racy reputation in the bustling market town thanks to her subscriptions to the *News of the World* tabloid newspaper and a naturist magazine called *Health and Efficiency*, which was widely regarded as pornographic. Roald also splashed out on an early black and white television set and for a time the two of them were very content in their new home, which was large enough for Roald to have his own entrance and the privacy he needed.

Sofie still demanded to know why her son refused to get married however, and could not begin to fathom his ongoing womanising ways, particularly when he took his nephews' Norwegian nanny sightseeing in London and she returned telling everyone about the size of the baths at the Savoy Hotel.

But seeing the payments starting to trickle into his bank account boosted Roald's spirits immeasurably; it meant he would not need to take the boring desk job he dreaded. With his stockbroking career on ice, he used what spare cash he had to indulge his great passion for greyhound racing. With money to spare he started buying dogs, and soon was the proud owner of sixteen racing dogs and even hired his own a trainer for them. Roald later confessed that he had blown £5,000 of his father's trust fund on dog racing, but the investment proved a wise one and to his delight the dogs were soon earning their keep and Roald was collecting substantial winnings at the race track. He adored the animals and remained an enthusiastic supporter of the sport for the rest of his life.

Roald had suffered his fair share of stinging criticism and harsh setbacks but felt his luck was changing at last, and was determined to write a new novel with no mention of flying, nor of RAF pilots or their grieving mothers, he did not want to focus on his own bleak sense of self-destruction or any of his usual ominous predictions for the future. He wanted to write something light-hearted for a change and chose as his subjects the eccentric bunch of misfit characters he was meeting as he explored the somewhat murky world of greyhound racing. He could not wait to get started and plunged himself into a comic look at the gamblers, breeders, antique dealers and poachers he knew in the English countryside.

Roald set to work with great enthusiasm in May 1948 but two years later he had only written a couple of chapters of *Fifty Thousand Frogskins*, having suffered a crippling bout of writer's block, or as he called it 'imaginative constipation'. He was the first to admit that he could be terribly lazy, and easily distracted by jobs that needed to be done in the garden, or by his pack of dogs, but also being forced to wear an uncomfortable back brace to ease the relentless pain made writing uncomfortable. He tried so hard to stay focused on the task in hand that even when Charles Marsh offered him another exotic holiday in 1949 he refused, saying he needed to finish the novel and admitting he was 'lazy enough already'.

Despite the slow progress, Roald laboured on with the novel which was to eventually become a comic and gossipy look at the friends he made in Great Missenden between 1946 and 1950. Among the characters who were an inspiration to Roald at the time was a local handyman called Claud Taylor who helped him build a customised writing desk out of a board cut from a green baize billiard table which could be placed across the arms of a large armchair, finally allowing him to write in comfort. He was so tall that standard desks were awkward for him, and the back brace meant ordinary office chairs were impossible. He would continue to use the same desk for the rest of his life, along with the same yellow lined legal pads and Dixon Ticonderoga pencils, which he always kept sharpened and stacked in even numbers because he believed odd numbers were unlucky.

On the surface Roald and Claud appeared to have little in common, but the two men shared a love of nature, gambling and poaching, and although they came from vastly different backgrounds they soon became constant companions as they tried to devise increasingly elaborate Get-Rich-Quick schemes together. Roald knew what they were doing was immoral, if not downright illegal, but was undeniably thrilled to be embroiled in what he described as Claud's ideas 'to acquire something by stealth without paying for it'. The chief victim of their schemes was usually Claud's unwitting boss George Brazil, a wealthy landowner who fell foul of their most notorious late-night plot. They worked a convoluted plan to lace raisins with sleeping pills and feed them to Brazil's pheasants, then wait until the birds passed out and caught them as they fell from the trees. Roald was so delighted with this ingenious scam that he recounted it many years later in *Danny The Champion of the World*. At the time he justified his questionable moral stance in a letter to Ann Watkins, explaining it was the best way for the birds to go: 'If anyone poached me, that's how I'd like it to be done.'

Claud was a keen gambler too. Roald had first felt the thrill of beating the odds in Washington where a clerk at the British Embassy had invited him to join twice-weekly games of bridge and poker at the exclusive University Club where members included high profile judges, a number of influential senators and even the future President Harry Truman. Roald was often unsuccessful at the card tables, but by then he had caught the bug. He found he got the same buzz from the unlicensed and secretive dog racing events that Claud took him to under the cloak of darkness in the fields around Buckinghamshire. He loved discovering these covert 'flapping tracks' and talked nostalgically about those nights until his death. Much of his enjoyment came when he realised that everyone there was an outsider, and he felt at home among these rootless people who shared his defiance of authority and bureaucracy. It started a lifelong admiration for what he saw as the freedom and subversion of the gypsy lifestyle.

Roald was still labouring over *Fifty Thousand Frogskins* which ended up littered with small time crooks in trilby hats, furtive spivs who traded on the black market, and wheeler-dealer bookmakers. The main characters, Hawes and Cubbage, dreamt up scams to make themselves a fortune at the expense of their enemies who tended to be tyrannical bureaucrats and university-educated intellectuals. Together they acquired two greyhounds, one of which was a born loser and the other a natural racer. They devised a plot to pass one off as the other and make money from the long betting odds, and despite various attempts to foil their plans the pair eventually triumphed.

While progress continued slowly on *Fifty Thousand Frogskins*, Roald was also working on a number of short stories, including *The Sound Machine* which was based on one he had first written at the age of 10. In his original schoolboy version a child discovers his uncle invented a machine for listening to past conversations and used it to prove a murder. Forty years later it was updated to become the story of a man who invented a similar device to listen to the sounds of trees and plants – including screams of pain as a result of human cruelty. He was brimming with ideas, and whenever they came to him, Roald tended to jot down a few unpunctuated words, perhaps a paragraph or even a sketch on a scrap of paper. Sometimes they were fleshed out into stories and others were not discovered until after his death. Some ideas were funny in the traditional sense, but he was also developing the rather grotesque and dark sense of humour which would become his trademark. His tales at this time included one about a man who ate his aunt's ashes by mistake, a man who grew a cherry the size of a grapefruit, as well as various weird and wonderful ways of murdering people without being detected – such as giving a diabetic too much sugar, tickling someone with a weak heart, murdering someone with a frozen leg of lamb and then roasting the evidence.

Roald often jotted down notes about the appearances of people he saw on the train or in newspapers, particularly if they seemed strange or ugly to him. He was especially fascinated by the look of murderers or children who inflicted cruelty on animals, and saved them as blueprints for sinister characters which would appear in his future stories.

Roald had a longed for ambition to see his work published in *The New Yorker* which had been his favourite magazine for years, and the delight he felt when *The Sound Machine* was accepted in 1949 soon turned to bitter rage when the editor Harold Ross dared to suggest various rewrites and a number of cuts. Roald fired back an indignant letter, saying he would prefer to abandon writing fiction altogether than become 'a sort of literary whore who will sleep with any editor however ugly his face'.

Standing up to such an influential figure in the publishing world was an extraordinary gamble for such an inexperienced writer to take and it could have killed Roald's career almost before it began, but Ross was pleasantly surprised at having his opinions challenged and backed down. Roald's arrogance paid off and Ross agreed to publish the original piece in full. Roald was triumphant, but his moment of glory was short lived as he struggled to get the story published in Britain. A string of rejection letters swiftly landed on his doorstep, and it would be a year before he saw another word in print again.

He consoled himself with his greyhounds and spent hours building model aeroplanes with his young nieces and nephews who adored their energetic and seemingly carefree uncle. But Roald was frustrated, money was becoming tight, and once again he had the creeping fear that it might be time to find himself a proper job.

He missed having enough spare cash to treat his family, as he had been able to do when he was in America. During the war he enjoyed being in a position to send food parcels home, but now he was having trouble supporting himself and his mother. Intending to use his love of gambling and greyhound racing, Roald thought he could set himself up as an independent bookmaker in London, taking bets on horses and dogs, but the plan was waylaid when he was offered an opportunity to deal in antiques and valuable paintings instead. Charles Marsh contacted Roald explaining that he and a number of his wealthy friends needed someone to scour art galleries in London looking for pieces they could acquire as investments.

Roald assured them he was the perfect man for the job. He had always been intrigued by the tricks of the art market, and his natural cynicism served him well as he became a fixture on the art scene. He quickly struck up a surprising new friendship with the elderly painter Matthew Smith. Smith was a virtual recluse but he was impressed when Roald tracked him down and agreed to help him search for artworks, which could be sold on for large profits. Perhaps recognising a kindred spirit in Roald, they were a tonic for each other's social lives and started going out on the town together too. Roald was enormously impressed with Smith's great stamina for sexual conquests, and watched closely how he flirted with women until he was well into his eighties. Roald told how he 'fornicates five times a week', and in a startling letter to Charles Marsh, Roald revealed:

> He walked the full length of Bayswater Road conversing with the whores. Matthew chased a black one six blocks, and when he caught up with her she said, 'You want to come home with me?' Matthew said, 'Have a cigarette.' 'Let's not fuck about,' the woman said. 'Do you or do you not want to come home with me? It'll cost you two pounds.' Whereupon the celebrated painter peered closer at her in the darkness, lit a match held it up to her face and exclaimed, 'My God no.' When I left him he was travelling fast towards an enormous woman with yellow hair.

Smith took his young protégé on several buying trips to Paris and even invited him to sit for a portrait in his blue RAF uniform – one of the very few male portraits he ever painted – and there was a suggestion that the two may have become more than just friends. But when Smith's daughter Alice Kadel interviewed Roald after her father's death in 1959 he told her: 'There was nothing homosexual about it.' She later said that the thought had never actually crossed her mind, and she found Roald aggressive, unpleasant and cold.

Although Roald had already made a significant dent in the large trust fund which had been left to him by his father, there was enough remaining to launch his art dealing enterprise, and he explained many years later how it had worked:

> Each time I sold a short story, I would buy a picture. Then, because it took me so long to write another story, I would invariably have to sell the picture I had bought six months before. In those days fine pictures were inexpensive. Many paintings that today could be acquired only by millionaires decorated my walls for brief periods in the late forties – Matisses, enormous Fauve Rouaults, Soutines, Cezanne watercolours, Bonnards, Boudins, a Renoir, a Sisley, a Degas seascape and God knows what else.

Roald and his sister Alfhild even attempted to paint several forgeries, which are still owned by Roald's nephew Nicholas, who went on to become a highly respected art dealer himself. But Roald and Smith fell out when the artist accused him of stealing a missing painting, which he had in fact just sent away to be framed. At the time he had been keeping more than fifty paintings in his spare bedroom while a new studio near Roald's house, which Smith wanted to rent, was being renovated. Smith became convinced that Roald was trying to con him by selling the painting on to Charles Marsh, and Roald was so devastated by the accusations that he was ill for weeks. Smith eventually apologised for the misunderstanding but Roald was offended by his lack of loyalty and told him: 'I hope to hell I shall never be found either mean or cunning or greedy about money or possessions.'

Smith left the area and moved back to a studio in London. Their friendship never fully recovered, although the episode later inspired Roald to write two stories about artists. *Nunc Dimittis* was a sinister account of a famous portrait artist who paints his subjects in the nude, adding clothes later; while *Skin* told of an impoverished and tormented Parisian artist who was killed after agreeing to sell a portrait of his wife which was tattooed onto his back.

Both were rejected by magazine editors in London, further convincing Roald that he would have done better to stay in New York where he felt his work had been far more appreciated. His only real ally on the London literary scene at the time was the famous playwright Noel Coward who had enjoyed Roald's flying stories, and the pair got along well when they met in Washington. Roald had initially been rather wary of Coward, who had exaggerated his spying role when he worked for the BSC, but he was short of allies and needed the boost Coward was offering by publicly recommending Roald's stories to publishers. And so while the two writers appeared perfectly friendly in public, and Coward would tell people that he was a brilliant writer, when *Someone Like You* was published he branded Roald a misfit who had 'An underlying streak of cruelty and macabre unpleasantness, and a curiously adolescent emphasis on sex.' Coward mused in his private diaries: 'He has lived in America too long and caught some of the prevalent sex hysteria.'

Realising he had few true friends, Roald was lonely and longed to return to America where he felt all his closest confidantes were. He was in constant contact with Charles Marsh who encouraged his writing, often lent him money, and told him: 'I am so very fond of you that I refuse to be merely your papa. My measure is that your spirit is with me now and tomorrow and yesterday.' They exchanged gossipy letters every week, sometimes discussing politics, work, their families and pets but more often their correspondence was made up of hilarious spoofs and jokes written under pseudonyms they dreamt up such as Charlie Suet from the Bureau of British Bullshit, Henry the Rubber, the Queen's hairy lady in waiting Eurydice Hislop Pomfret Pomfret, Investigator Fingerfucker, and Detectives Slobgollion and Worms of Scotland Yard.

During these years of post-war austerity in Britain, Charles also showered Roald and his family with food, clothes and new electrical gadgets, but on the several occasions when he flew over to visit the Dahls in Buckinghamshire, the rest of the family were reluctant to accept his gifts. They found him pushy and patronising, and feared he was trying to lure their brother back to the States for good.

Charles encouraged his friend to let him know about any cases of hardship he came across, which he could help with financial grants, food or whatever else was required. Charles sent much needed food supplies to undernourished Londoners in Clement Atlee's East End constituency after Roald told him they had suffered the worst of the Blitz bombing.

Meanwhile Roald was still finding himself largely ignored by the British publishing and broadcasting worlds. He longed to have his work broadcast on the BBC, but was soon seething with resentment over the dismissive ways in which stories he submitted were rejected. He was having a little more luck across the Atlantic where the CBS network bought the radio and television rights for *The Sound Machine* thanks to Ann Watkins, but even she was starting to get frustrated by how slowly he seemed to be supplying her with new work.

Ann repeatedly urged Roald to be more productive but when he finally finished *Fifty Thousand Frogskins* in early 1951, he was so worried that she would not like it that he sent it straight to Peter Wyld at *Collins* magazine instead. The magazine rejected it instantly and Roald was left with no option but to send a copy to Ann. Nobody had seen a word of it apart from a girl in the village he had hired to type up the manuscript, and she had been, 'In turn disgusted, horrified, amused, then disgusted again.'

Ann was furious that her client had attempted to bypass her in such an unprofessional way. It was her job to pass Roald's manuscripts on to magazine editors, and she sent him a blunt telegram saying: 'FROGSKINS UNPUBLISHABLE IN PRESENT FORM. CONSTRUCTION UNSOUND. TOO MANY LOOSE ENDS.' She followed that message up with a critical letter describing the novel as 'dull and not nearly good enough'.

CHAPTER SEVEN

Mortified, Roald fled to Lebanon and sent Ann a postcard when he reached Beirut saying: 'I have not read your letter. I have not dared to read it. Perhaps it's chasing me. But I don't think it will ever catch me because I am moving fast.' Of course Charles Marsh was there to save Roald in his hour of need, sweeping him back to New York where he insisted he take refuge in his lavish apartment and swiftly secured Roald both a job and a visa so he could stay as long as he needed to recover from the mess. Humiliated by the rejection, Roald destroyed all the letters from Ann and Peter Wyld, some of them not even opened, and ignored pleas from his mother and sister to return home.

He should have enjoyed being back among his glamorous friends in Manhattan but Roald's spirits were low. He was 36-years-old, living with his mother and relying on the generosity of a wealthy benefactor.

Charles decided that what Roald really needed was a wife.

Chapter Eight

Roald never seemed to have much trouble attracting women, but he had yet to meet anyone who seemed marriage material. Charles did his best to match-make, by introducing him to wealthy and well connected women who moved in his circles. By the autumn of 1951 Roald had fallen in love with Suzanne Horvath, a Hungarian divorcee who impressed him by beating him at chess, and any money he made by selling paintings he would spend on expensive gifts for Suzanne. Soon he was spending so much time with her, and his mother heard from Roald so rarely, that she feared they had actually got married in secret. It was February 1952 before he finally put Sofie's mind at rest by admitting he was getting cold feet and did not intend to make any commitment for a very long time. When Suzanne ended the romance a few months later, Sofie wrote: 'Roald is not rich enough for keeping a divorced wife. I was not surprised as I had not expected it to come off.'

Far from being left heartbroken over the split, Roald soon found himself captivated by a glamorous young Hollywood starlet. Patricia Neal had just ended her three-year affair with Gary Cooper and fled Los Angeles, distraught because her famous movie-star lover had abandoned her. After discovering that Patricia was pregnant, Cooper had returned to his wife and insisted on a termination.

Her acting career appeared to be lying in tatters too. Although she had appeared in thirteen films, including two with Ronald Reagan, Patricia had not fulfilled the early signs of promise that Warner Bros had hoped for and the studio terminated her initial contract. In a desperate bid for the stardom she craved, Patricia had been performing a series of gruelling live shows for US troops stationed in Korea, and, on the verge of a complete emotional and physical breakdown, she decided to take refuge among friends in Manhattan before returning to face the music in California.

Despite having lost much of her former confidence, Patricia decided to go ahead with an audition for the Broadway producer Lillian Hellman who was shocked by how gaunt the actress looked and immediately invited her

Right: Roald and his first wife Patricia Neal. They were married from 1953 to 1983 and had five children, Olivia, Tessa, Ophelia, Theo and Lucy. (Public Domain)

Below: Mrs Pratchett's sweetshop, now a Chinese takeaway, in Llandaff, scene of the Great Mouse Plot of 1924, when Roald and his friends hid a dead mouse in a jar of gobstoppers. An historic blue plaque on the wall now commemorates the prank. (Public Domain)

Repton School in Derbyshire, which Roald attended from 1929 to 1934. (Public Domain)

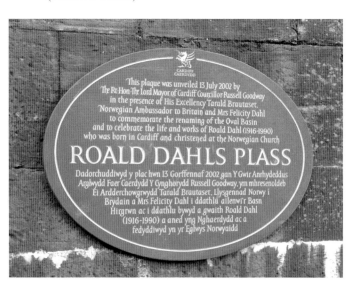

The Roald Dahl Plass in Cardiff (plass means place or square), marking Roald's Norwegian heritage. (Public Domain)

Above: Roald was flying a Gloster Gladiator when he crashed in Libya in September 1940, leaving him with lifelong spinal injuries. (Public Domain)

Right: Roald's RAF uniform, now on display at the Roald Dahl Museum and Story Centre in Great Missenden, Buckinghamshire. Roald lived in the village for thirty-six years until his death in 1990. (Author's own collection)

Roald wrote seven days a week in this unassuming hut, which he had specially built at the bottom of the garden at Gipsy House, far from the noise of his young family. (Author's own collection)

Dylan Thomas's shed. Roald was inspired to install his famous writing hut after visiting this one, belonging to one of his favourite authors. (Author's own collection)

Above: Great Missenden Library where *Matilda*, his most beloved female character, falls in love with reading after her mother leaves her there while she plays bingo. (Author's own collection)

Right: The 1950s-style petrol filling station, which was the inspiration for the garage in *Danny Champion of the World*. Just a little further along the High Street is Crown House, the timber framed house on which he based Sophie's orphanage in *The BFG*. (Author's own collection)

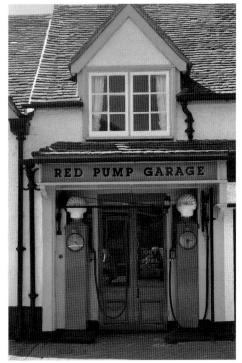

Above: The Roald Dahl Museum and Story Centre in Great Missenden, which now welcomes over 150,000 visitors a year from across the globe. (Author's own collection)

Left: The chocolate door in the museum, which is full of photos and facts about Roald's fascinating life. (Author's own collection)

Above: One of the sets from *Fantastic Mr Fox*, the hit film starring George Clooney and Meryl Streep, on display at The Roald Dahl Museum and Story Centre. (Author's own collection)

Right: Giant feet lead visitors across St Peter and St Paul's Church in Great Missenden to Roald's grave. (Author's own collection)

Roald's grave. He is buried next to his step-daughter Lorina, and fans still leave flowers, toys, chocolate and even onions as they were his favourite vegetable. (Author's own collection)

Matilda is Roald's most lucrative story to date. *Matilda the Musical* has been shown in London's West End since November 2011 and on Broadway in New York since April 2013. (Author's own collection)

to dinner. Roald happened to be among the guests, and there was an instant spark between them. Highly eligible but nursing broken hearts, they both felt it was time to settle down, marry someone suitable, and have children. Roald's first impression of Patricia was how sad she seemed: 'She was reserved, holding herself in; obviously pretty shaken all round. Think she planned to work hard as an antidote to her personal misfortunes. It wasn't a happy girl I was seeing,' he recalled later.

Patricia said she noticed Roald as soon as he walked in, but he completely ignored her and spent most of the evening chatting to the musician Leonard Bernstein. Patricia decided he was intolerably rude and she hated him, so when he phoned her the following morning to ask her out on a date, she refused. But two days later he tried again, and this time she accepted, hoping he might make a much more suitable match than the Hollywood playboys she had been dating.

Their first date was a huge success, they talked for hours about paintings and antiques, and Roald told her all about his love of the English countryside. Roald even took her to meet Charles Marsh who was so delighted he apparently whispered: 'Drop the other baggage, I like this one!' As usual Roald was secretive with his family, but after a few months the press had caught wind of their romance, and Roald sent his mother a cutting from a newspaper gossip column, which reported 'Patricia Neal is now adored by Roald Dahl'.

Sofie was baffled and full of questions about his new celebrity status and although Roald refused to supply his family with any further details, the relationship was clearly heading in the right direction. When Patricia saw photographs of his nieces and nephews, she decided they would 'make beautiful children', although later suspected he had left the pictures out for her to find deliberately hoping they would have that effect: 'He knew exactly what he wanted and he went quietly about getting it,' she said.

Patricia looked happier and more energised than she had in quite some time, but seemed reluctant to commit to Roald or admit it was serious, and friends feared she was still pining after Cooper. Luckily Charles Marsh took it upon himself to intervene and urged Roald to speed things along. One night, after a performance of her Broadway show *The Children's Play*, Roald proposed in her dressing room, but to his amazement she turned him down. He was shocked and confused, but a few weeks later she changed her mind.

Patricia explained: 'I did want marriage. And a family. Roald would have beautiful children. What was I holding out for? A great love? That would never come again. When was I going to face reality?'

Roald excitedly shared the news with his mother, boasting about how much Patricia was earning in her play and explaining that he would be bringing his fiancé home to meet the family that summer, after shipping a convertible Jaguar car from New York to Rome which they would then drive slowly back through France to England. He failed to mention in the letter written in May 1956 that the trip was actually going to be their honeymoon, and they married in a low-key ceremony at Trinity Church near Wall Street just six weeks later on 2 July.

Charles Marsh had given Roald a huge sapphire ring to present to his wife, agreed to be best man, and offered to host the reception at his apartment, but before the wedding had even taken place, the couple were already fighting.

Patricia's friend Leonard Bernstein warned she was 'making the biggest mistake of her life,' but she was desperate to prove to the world that she had moved on from Cooper. Days before they tied the knot Patricia accused Roald of being rude and arrogant towards her friends and threatened to call off the wedding unless he apologised. He refused and eventually she backed down.

Then Patricia said she wanted to get married in a church, which Roald thought was a ridiculous idea, although he agreed to her request on the condition that she slashed the guest list. He hated the idea of a showbiz circus full of strangers even more than he hated the idea of saying his vows in a church. Patricia was worried that her family would be offended at not being invited so Roald agreed to write to her mother Eura, explaining that there would not be any members of either family there as they did not want any fuss. Sofie was alone in her cottage, more than 3,000 miles away when her only son and his Hollywood starlet were pronounced man and wife.

In the end Patricia was glad nobody was there to see her husband tearing at the beautiful suit she had bought him because the silk lining was too hot. And some years later Patricia revealed that she had secretly cried on her wedding night, regretting marrying Roald and fervently wishing she was still with Gary Cooper. The honeymoon was also a disaster, plagued with bad omens for the future. Roald had borrowed thousands of pounds to pay for the trip to Europe, but the car kept breaking down and Patricia showed almost no interest in the art and architecture he had been looking forward to showing her. Her mood improved a little when they reached England and Roald's family took an immediate liking to his new bride – although at first Sofie was appalled that her daughter-in-law slept all morning and could not cook; looking back on their visit she wrote: 'We all love her, and think that she couldn't possibly be nicer and hope that she and Roald will be happy together. We all missed them when they went.'

Patricia loved the Dahl clan's close-knit family unit, but Roald was not so impressed with the Neals when he met them all in Georgia following their honeymoon. Roald hid in his room, only appeared for meals, and wrote to his mother: 'They're all very pleasant but pretty dull. I wasn't sorry to leave.'

By the time the newlyweds returned to New York, Patricia was already complaining bitterly that her husband was not bringing in a regular salary, and she had no choice but to be the main breadwinner: 'It was my money when we were married. Roald didn't have any money at all,' she said.

Patricia may have been having her doubts, but married life suited Roald and while he could not be quite sure whether it was his star status or his improved creativity that sealed it, he sold several stories to *The New Yorker* magazine. They bought several in quick succession – *Taste, My Lady Love, Skin* and *My Dove*. They were dark and grisly tales, but readers loved them and the magazine asked to be the first to see any short stories Roald wrote in the future. After years of being left in the wilderness by the British publishing industry, Roald was being recognised in America again, giving him a new glimmer of hope. His deal with *The New Yorker* also meant he could afford to rent his own apartment, rather than relying on the endless support of Charles Marsh. It felt like a fresh start, and feeling more energetic than he had in years, Roald quickly established a daily routine, determined to treat writing as a full time job from now on, rather than an occasional hobby he dabbled in.

Before long his work was really gathering momentum in America. *Someone Like You*, his most recent collection of short stories, received glowing reviews and the initial print run of 5,000 sold out within a week. After a few months sales had topped 25,000 copies.

Roald's career may have been starting to flourish, but his marriage was not. It was already obvious how little he and Patricia had in common, they were both used to their independence and struggled to adapt to sharing their living space. Roald needed peace to write, but she was used to being the centre of attention. Her fame irritated him, particularly as he was usually referred to simply as 'the husband of Patricia Neal'; or if his name was used it was often misspelt. Roald longed to return to the tranquillity of the English countryside to start a family, but the thought left Patricia cold. Roald told Charles and Claudia Marsh, their best friends, that there were simply far too many differences for the couple to ever be truly compatible – they rarely talked, and evenings spent alone tended to be awkward. He enjoyed reading quietly, while Patricia preferred nights out with her theatrical friends who Roald blatantly could not stand. He had also become irritated by her inability to prepare meals or take on any traditional domestic duties while he worked.

He felt that she was far too focused on her acting career to be a 'normal wife', and any attempts to change her would ultimately be doomed to fail.

Rumours were soon swirling about Roald having an affair with society heiress Gloria Vanderbilt, and at Christmas 1955 Roald told Patricia that he wanted a divorce. She told how he had broken the devastating news to her quite nonchalantly in bed one night, adding: 'Don't worry about it now, just go to sleep.' She was not prepared to give up quite so easily and flew to Jamaica where she hoped Charles and Claudia could help her understand how her marriage had gone so badly wrong so quickly. They already knew all about their troubles, as Roald had been confiding his most intimate thoughts in his regular long letters, and the couple also doubted that the marriage would ever actually work. Roald wrote:

> Whichever way I look at it and however hard I try to change my own mind, I still always come to the same conclusion – that I do not believe it is possible for us to live together in complete serenity. She is still far and away the nicest girl I know and is full of the two great qualities – courage and honesty. But that doesn't necessarily mean that we shall feel comfortable and as it were complete in each other's company.
>
> It seems horrid to be enumerating these little things, but they are the things that start the resentments building up inside one. She is naturally absorbed in herself because she is a fine and successful actress, but I do not believe it is possible to be a successful wife and to be absorbed in yourself at the same time unless you are very clever.

Roald longed to become a father, but realised that it would be wrong for him and Patricia to carry on trying for a baby when the relationship was so clearly doomed: 'It would be unkind and foolish to deceive, or to prolong something that must, so far as I can see, gradually fail in the end. It's probably all my fault,' he wrote. Charles urged Roald not to blame himself, but all their friends could clearly see the marriage had no future. Roald joined his wife in Jamaica when Charles was taken seriously ill with malaria, and the time spent together forced them to revaluate their priorities. Charles's brush with death put things into perspective for Roald; he was terrified at the idea of losing his best friend and mentor and pledged to put more effort into his troubled marriage. He ended his affair with Gloria Vanderbilt, and Patricia agreed to try harder with the domestic side of things.

Having patched up some of their differences at least, the couple returned to New York together happier than they had seemed in months. They opened a joint bank account and visited a specialist gynaecologist to find out why, after nine months of marriage, Patricia was still not pregnant. She was treated for blocked fallopian tubes and they agreed to find a way to satisfy his urge to return to rural England – the compromise was that they would spend the summer months in Buckinghamshire and return to New York every winter. Sofie was thrilled to be getting her son back, at least part of the time, and found them an idyllic looking cottage near Great Missenden, which they bought for £4,000 without even seeing it. Six weeks later they arrived to redecorate, and during one of their many long walks exploring the fields surrounding the cottage, Patricia finally conceived. At the end of July 1954 they moved into their newly renovated cottage, Little Whitefield – with a little Dahl on the way – and for the first time in months Roald felt positive about their marriage and excited about the future.

Chapter Nine

Sales of *Someone Like You* were moving slowly in Britain and Roald was frustrated by the lack of enthusiasm shown by his publishers and agents when it came to marketing and advertising. The reviews were generally favourable, particularly one from *Time and Tide* magazine which accurately predicted: 'Mr Dahl behaves in his work like the mad inventor of a book for boys.'

Indeed Roald was already showing a remarkable ability to enter the minds of young children and after reading *The Rock*, his short story about a boy who convinces himself that treading on various patches of carpet will take him into a black hole or be poisoned by snakes, his new American publisher Sheila St Lawrence urged Roald to write a full length children's book. He was forming a close working relationship with Sheila because her boss Ann Watkins was starting to take a back seat with her clients as she prepared to retire, and had asked Sheila to take over Roald's literary affairs. She was a good choice and Roald liked her immediately. Sheila was younger than him, gossipy and direct, and Roald soon relied on her advice as heavily as he once had on Ann's.

He liked Sheila's idea of writing for children, but that summer Roald was far too busy working on a film script of Herman Melville's classic novel *Moby Dick*. With a baby on the way, Roald was only doing it for the money since he found the process of screenwriting irritatingly slow and laborious. He had similar reservations about theatrical scripts but despite his reservations, Sheila persuaded him to work on an adaptation of three of his most macabre short stories. His first play, *The Honeys*, which would eventually be produced in London and New York was about a woman driven to murder her three husbands. Roald argued relentlessly with the American producers from the start and objected to their casting. The show was a flop when it opened on Broadway, and after dire reviews it closed early. In London's West End he had to endure a similar humiliation all over again, and when the producers demanded yet more rewrites, Roald was desperate to abandon the entire project and blamed the cast for its failure. The timing of his play could not have been worse as it clashed with the premiere of John Osborne's *Look Back In Anger* which ushered in a new wave of gritty, angry realism in British theatre, and sinister stories like Roald's were unfashionable.

It was time to move on, and Sheila urged him once again to think about stories for children: 'It seems perhaps the time has come to divorce yourself from it and start afresh with the stories that we as well as your reading public are clamouring for.' Children were very much on his mind at home too. Roald enjoyed watching the baby bump grow on Patricia, who he started affectionately calling Old Sausage, and when their daughter Olivia Twenty was born on 20 April 1955 during a trip to New York, she was named after Patricia's favourite Shakespeare character and her date of birth. Roald would later claim her unusual middle name was chosen because he had $20 in his pocket when he arrived at the hospital.

A few weeks later they returned to Great Missenden for the summer but Patricia found motherhood difficult, convinced that Olivia was 'at war' with her, or 'lying in wait' to start screaming whenever she came near. Soon, much of the baby's care was left to her sister-in-law Else Logsdail who was wonderfully calm with her niece. Roald on the other hand loved being a father, and did not object when his wife accepted a role in new film called *A Face In The Crowd* which would mean her being away from the baby for five months, leaving him with very little time to write. Patricia was already pregnant again by the time she left to start filming, but he did not stop her, and instead minimised the disruption by hiring a nanny and ordering himself a writing hut. Roald remembered that one of his literary heroes, Welsh poet Dylan Thomas, wrote in a small garden shed so he travelled to Carmarthenshire to take a look inside it for himself. He thought it was perfect and recreated the same arrangement at the bottom of his garden, as far away from all the noise in the house as possible.

As he explained to Sheila, who had also recently had her first child:

> There's no doubt that babies are charming, but they do bugger
> up the quiet and routine necessary for work. Between you and
> me I can do without the little buggers until they are six months
> old. Until then they are nothing but a great whirling blur of wet
> nappies and vomit and milk and belching and farting.

That summer Roald was reunited with his mischievous old pal Claud Taylor, and it was not long before the pair were up to their old tricks again, and hatching schemes against local landowners. Late one night they decided to see if they could make a prize Black Angus bull mate with some of Claud's small herd of cows. Roald loved recounting the hilarious escapade which also appeared much later in his novel *My Uncle Oswald*.

For the next few years the Dahls stuck to their agreement and divided their time between Buckinghamshire and their apartment on Manhattan's Upper East Side, with stints in Hollywood if Patricia's schedule demanded it. Patricia carried on working as much as she could, fitting filming around two further pregnancies. A second daughter Chantal Sophia was born in Oxford in April 1957 but when Roald realised that Chantal rhymed with Dahl, he quickly changed her name to Tessa. Then in July 1960 their son Theo arrived, and the three toddlers made so much noise that Roald ended up renting a room in a different apartment to escape when he needed to work. With Patricia away so much Roald was responsible for the bulk of the childcare but he was having trouble concentrating and *The New Yorker* appeared to have gone cold on him, with editors demanding time-consuming rewrites before eventually turning the stories down. He submitted his stories far and wide and had some surprising success with *Playboy* magazine, but was in no position to turn down any offers, even if they were from pornographic publications.

Roald could not find pleasure in Manhattan. He loathed the frantic pace of city life and found his stories were becoming even darker and more grisly than before. He longed to settle permanently back in Britain, and hated the idea of raising his family among the noise and traffic of a busy city like New York, but whether he liked it or not his wife was by far the main earner and her work was in America. *A Face In The Crowd* was a box office triumph when it was released, and signified Patricia's return to the mainstream superstar status she had feared was lost forever. It also meant even more time away from the family, leaving Roald unsettled, lonely and lacking in focus. He had started jotting down random ideas which could have become the plot of a children's story but told Sheila he was 'Not so much depressed now as puzzled. I shall not write any more stories.' She urged him to find a fresh challenge to invigorate his imagination. Roald had always enjoyed making up stories for his friends' children, and always held them spellbound with the fanciful tales he spun off the top of his head. Now he had children of his own, and since Roald was usually the one to put them to bed each night, he found himself revisiting his own childhood favourites.

He enjoyed reading Olivia, Tessa and Theo traditional Norwegian fairy tales, the Brothers Grimm, Beatrix Potter and Hilaire Belloc's *Cautionary Tales*. But Roald and the children enjoyed bedtime the most when he would make up stories of his own. His adult stories had been chilling and fearful, but now his storytelling style was gradually changing. He was beginning to feature children as the main protagonists.

He may not have realised it at the time, but Roald was taking the first steps towards the work that would ultimately define him and become his life's legacy. His pencil jottings from late 1959 and early 1960 include 'tiny humans in hollow tree,' 'child who dreamed of the future which always came true', and 'child who could move objects'. But he did not have a firm idea of what exactly he wanted to write about, and was hesitant to get started.

He knew from his own children that stories involving animal characters would be popular, and he started to slowly flesh out the idea of a story about insects. Of course he knew there were already far too many children's books about smiling puppies, ducks and rabbits, so he wanted to write about the tiny insignificant animals such as worms, centipedes and spiders who were eating the fruit trees in his garden. For a while he mulled over the idea of the chief child character becoming very small, or the insects becoming very large, so they could relate to each other. One day he struck upon the idea of the characters being insects living inside enormous fruits, and decided a peach would work best because they were rare at the time and their flavour seemed the most exciting.

That summer the family went on holiday to Norway, and it was there that Roald wrote *James and the Giant Peach*, the story of an orphaned boy sent to live with two cruel aunts, Aunt Sponge and Aunt Spiker, after his parents were killed – in the second paragraph of the book – by an angry rhinoceros that has escaped from the zoo.

The nasty old hags, who beat and starved him mercilessly, were crushed by an enormous peach when it fell from a tree full of insects, and James was whisked away on a series of exciting adventures with his new creepy crawly friends. Carried by seagulls holding threads spun by silkworms, the peach flew across the Atlantic Ocean before finally landing on the top of the needle of the Empire State Building in New York.

Roald was delighted to finally have the story mapped out in his mind, but progress was slow initially since he ended up spending much of the summer indulging his hobby of buying and selling antiques and developing a proposal to create a drama series out of twenty-four classic ghost stories for American television. When that project was soon shelved, Roald was left with little choice but to return to *James and the Giant Peach*.

He threw himself in vividly describing Aunt Sponge and Aunt Spiker who became the first of many of Roald's grotesque villains. He discovered a remarkable talent for describing the most unpleasant characters with a gleeful relish which would soon become well known as his very distinctive style, employed to devastating effect particularly when he was writing about cruel and selfish women. He wrote:

> Aunt Sponge was enormously fat and very short. She had small piggy eyes, a sunken mouth, and one of those white flabby faces that looked exactly as though it had been boiled. She was like a great white, soggy over boiled cabbage. Aunt Spiker, on the other hand, was lean and tall and bony, and she wore steel-rimmed spectacles that fixed on to the end of her nose with a clip. She had a screeching voice and long, wet, narrow lips, and whenever she got angry or excited, little flecks of spit would come shooting out of her mouth as she talked.

The first person he let read *James and the Giant Peach* was Patricia, who loved it, followed by Sheila who was equally enthusiastic about the pages when they landed on her desk. She saw it as his best literary submission to date, and immediately sent back extra ideas, notes and all kinds of imaginative new details for Roald to incorporate into his next draft. She was convinced she had a best seller on her hands and after reading the second draft she wrote to her star author: 'Really, honestly, truly it is unbelievably better than ever, and better than I ever thought it could be. I think you've done the undoable, crossed the border between adult and juvenile.'

Sheila was right of course, and Roald had his first major hit on his hands.

Chapter Ten

The start of the Sixties looked set to be a golden time for the Dahl family. Roald had scored not one but two hits – *James and the Giant Peach* was being hailed as good as other classic children's stories including *Charlotte's Web* and *Stuart Little*, and his new adult novel *Kiss Kiss* was becoming a bestseller too. As he set sail from Manhattan to spend the summer in England he noticed that many of his fellow passengers on board the ship were reading copies of *Kiss Kiss*. He felt elated to be returning with Olivia, Tessa and Theo who loved being surrounded by their relatives in the countryside. Roald's nieces Anna and Lou Logsdail helped out with the children, and with his elderly mother living just five minutes away, he could visit her every day. He bought a traditional gypsy caravan for the children to use as a playhouse in the garden, and renamed their home Gipsy House. London was only an hour away so he could easily travel to and from meetings.

The only blot on the landscape was a rift between him and his American agent Sheila St Lawrence when Roald decided, to her surprise, she was not the best person to negotiate the translation rights to either *Kiss Kiss* or *James and the Giant Peach* for him. Instead Roald started to work with Laurence Pollinger, a London-based literary agent who had impressed him with his brisk and efficient attitude. He felt Pollinger was better placed geographically to handle the European territories but Sheila, who was grieving the death of her father, was furious at what she saw as a huge betrayal after thirteen years of loyal friendship and unswerving professional support. After an explosive exchange of letters, Roald eventually apologised for upsetting her and questioning her abilities, but was too stubborn to change his mind on the matter. It did blow over, but Sheila passed all his affairs to Mike Watkins who had taken over the running of the agency from his mother, Roald's former agent Ann.

The highlight of that idyllic summer in England had of course been the birth of Roald and Pat's son, Theo Matthew. Roald was thrilled and fascinated by the arrival of the first male in the family and wrote: 'He has a pair of testicles the size of walnuts and a sharp wicked penis. He's a fine nipper, and his circumcised tool (now healed) glows with promise, like the small unopened bud of some exotic flower.'

Six weeks later, the family returned to New York for the winter. Roald stuck to the agreement he had made with his wife, but he was doing it increasingly grudgingly with every passing year. He disliked the city more and more each time they returned, he found it threatening, violent and aggressive. And his very worst fears were realised on 5 December 1960 when Theo's pram was hit by a taxi on the corner of a busy Manhattan street and his head was crushed into the side of a bus. Theo's nanny Susan Denton had just collected the baby from nursery and was pushing him home for lunch when the cab careered around the corner of Madison Avenue and 85th Street and smashed into the pram. The driver panicked and accelerated instead of braking, which threw the pram forty feet into the air before it fell against the side of a parked bus. Theo's head took the full force of the impact which left his skull shattered. Both Roald and Pat, who were nearby at the time, heard the sirens but had no idea it was their son being rushed to Lenox Hill Hospital, along with his sister Tessa and their dog Stormy. Theo was diagnosed with such a severe neurological deficit that doctors were in no doubt that he would die.

Various surgeons rushed to examine the baby and although there was some disagreement over the best treatment to give him, he was quickly X-rayed and given plasma and a subdural tap to relieve the pressure on his brain. Roald was distraught yet somehow decided the best way to straighten out his jumbled thoughts would be to write down every tiny detail of the aftermath of the crash. *A Note on Theo's Accident* is an extraordinary account of the chaos of an emergency:

> I stayed all night in hospital watching the baby … At 1 a.m. his temperature went down to 101. At 2 a.m. it went to 99 and stayed there. He was still having blood and intravenous feeding. His blood count was low, indicating a big loss of blood somewhere. He was also in an oxygen tent. I had a row with nurses about fixing a catheter tube.

Roald meticulously described various disagreements between doctors over how best to treat Theo, culminating in an argument when a nurse accidentally gave Theo the wrong dose of a sedative. Furious, Roald insisted on moving their son to the neurological wing of Presbyterian Hospital, with the help of Pat's friend the actress Anne Bancroft and her agent Harvey Orkin. Theo was getting the best possible care, but weeks of uncertainty followed. The baby was in an oxygen tent for two weeks and required several operations to drain fluid from his brain. Although it looked as if he might survive, there was no way of knowing what the extent of his brain damage would be.

To make matters worse, the streets were icy and Roald slipped outside the hospital and broke his ankle, then caught flu and was confined to bed. Theo was allowed home for Christmas but on New Year's Eve their neighbour, psychiatrist Sonia Austrian, noticed he had become oddly quiet and slow to react, and she feared he had gone blind. Cerebrospinal fluid had built up in Theo's cranial cavity and was pressing on his brain, causing him to lose his sight. They rushed him back to hospital where the fluid was quickly drained but doctors warned that there was a risk the pressure could leave him permanently blind. Miraculously his sight returned over the next two weeks and Theo was declared fit enough to return home on 14 January, but soon started to deteriorate again as the internal drainage tube that had been fitted into his heart became blocked. Surgeons operated again and cleared the blockage which allowed his sight to return, but it was left greatly impaired. The same thing happened six more times over the next nine months and each time Theo endured an operation there was a chance he would be left blind or brain damaged.

Roald realised that defective valves were causing the problem and decided to research a way of improving the tiny plastic tubes being used to drain the fluid from his son's brain. He tracked down a Scottish neurosurgeon called Wylie McKissock who had performed similar operations using a different type of tube. When Theo had another relapse after the family had returned to England in May, McKissock agreed to travel south to fit the alternative valve but that one also failed to function effectively. Roald refused to give up, and threw himself into researching the subject, soon becoming something of an expert, before hitting on the idea of contacting a particularly creative toymaker he had met years earlier.

When he had bought a miniature steam train for his nephew Nicholas a decade earlier, Roald had been impressed by how much pride Stanley Wade appeared to take in perfecting the tiny toy engines. He described the toymaker as: 'A brilliant metal turner who could turn a minute steel component to an accuracy of ten thousandths of a millimetre.' As well as trains, Wade also specialised in making model aeroplanes with tiny hydraulic pumps to supply them with fuel, which was effectively what Theo needed. When Roald explained what was repeatedly happening to his son, Wade agreed to make a valve to his specific requirements. Theo's consultant at Great Ormond Street Hospital in London, Kenneth Till, agreed to let both Roald and Stanley Wade watch him perform an operation so that they could understand more precisely what was required from the mechanism. Strictly it was against hospital protocol, but Till had been impressed by Roald's cool and detached attitude to the problem.

Theo's condition did not improve that summer, and Roald struggled to write. He had rigged up a rudimentary communication system so Patricia could let him know if he was needed in the house. There was a switch in the house and a light bulb in his writing hut; one flash meant a minor disturbance, two flashes alerted him to an emergency.

In October 1961 the light flashed twice and Roald ran to the house. Theo's lung had collapsed and he was having difficulty breathing. They rushed him to hospital and yet again doctors warned that his chances of survival were slim, but a new tube was fitted to reduce the swelling on his brain. He was home again in January 1962 but his parents were in a constant state of high alert, waiting for the next crisis.

Roald, Stanley Wade and Kenneth Till redoubled their efforts to get their pioneering valve made, and by May that year the Dahl-Wade-Till (DWT) Valve was ready to be fitted on a child with the same life-threatening condition as Theo. Their invention was just two centimetres long but had six moving steel parts, and worked perfectly. The medical journal *The Lancet* reported it as a major surgical breakthrough, and since Dahl, Wade and Till had agreed that they did not want to make any money from their invention, it cost hospitals less than a third of any other similar product to fit. Thanks to Roald's insatiable curiosity and refusal to accept the situation, the DWT Valve was used successfully on almost 3,000 children around the world before it was replaced by a new version.

Roald continued to find aspects of the medical profession deeply fascinating for the rest of his life, particularly when he read about pioneering doctors who were discovering ground-breaking new ideas to cure illnesses. Indeed, he became such an expert in various medical procedures that when an airline steward asked if there was a doctor on board a long distance flight, Roald actually came forward and offered to help with the emergency.

But once the worst of Theo's trauma was over and it looked like he might make a far more promising recovery than anyone had dared to imagine, Roald craved the peace and tranquillity of the countryside more than ever. He was convinced that the hectic pace of life in New York had been to blame for Theo's accident, it would never have happened in rural England he felt, and he longed to move back to Great Missenden permanently where he could keep his family safe.

He also knew that he wrote best in his peaceful hut at the end of the garden at Gipsy House, which had been divided into two small six-foot wide rooms, one for storing his letters and files and the other held his leather armchair and makeshift writing desk. If left undisturbed for hours at a time, this was where Roald could actually allow his wild imagination to run free.

He knew sales of *James and the Giant Peach* would really soar if he found the illustrator he wanted; Roald was ahead of his time in understanding what a difference the artwork could make when it came to making children truly excited about a book. He spent months hoping to find someone like Ernest Shepard, the artist who had created Christopher Robin for A. A. Milne's popular *Winnie the Pooh* stories. He told his American editors that Christopher Robin 'is and always will be the perfect small boy. A face with character is not so important as a face with charm. One must fall in love with it.'

Once he finally agreed to give American painter Nancy Burkert the job, the book triumphed again with critics and readers alike, but in his mind Roald had already moved on to his next children's book. He was tinkering with the manuscript of a story called *Charlie's Chocolate Boy*, but his agent Mike Watkins was not easily impressed and told Roald it was 'Not quite up to the level of *James*.' Roald was stung by the sharp criticism and found himself longing for the easy and successful working relationship he had previously enjoyed with Watkins's predecessor, Sheila St Lawrence, and before her with Mike's mother Ann. Both women had long since retired from publishing, and Patricia was rarely around to give her husband advice either. He knew she would be able to give him the encouragement he needed to improve *Charlie's Chocolate Boy* but she was away filming in Texas with Hollywood hunk Paul Newman. Despite another lengthy separation, their marriage actually seemed stronger than ever. Sharing the trauma of looking after Theo had brought them closer since it made their own problems seem insignificant and Patricia admitted in an interview that she no longer wanted to 'have nice fights and make it up in bed'. They now trusted each other and agreed that making a real family home in England would be the best thing for the whole family.

At first Patricia missed her New York apartment, and Olivia and Tessa were unsettled at their new schools, but Roald did all he could to help them feel happy there – once he made their names magically appear on the lawn by sprinkling weed killer on the grass while they were asleep – and after a year none of them had any desire to return to the States at all. They were just starting to feel like a normal, happy family when the headmistress of Olivia's new school sent a letter to all the parents warning of an outbreak of measles encephalitis. In November 1962 there was no vaccination readily available to prevent measles. A medicine called gamma globulin could fight it, but was not offered to everyone and since Theo was so vulnerable to any risk of infection, they gave all the medicine they had to him.

Roald and Patricia were not unduly concerned when Olivia broke out in spots a few days later, and after three days the worst of her fever had subsided as expected, and she was sitting up in bed beating her father at chess. But the following morning she complained of a headache and said all she wanted to do was sleep. A doctor was called and agreed that Olivia was lethargic and should probably be left to sleep, but at 5 p.m. that day Patricia found her daughter having convulsions, before suddenly going completely still and limp. Patricia ran to the light switch that connected to a bulb in Roald's writing hut, and sent four quick flashes. Two flashes meant an emergency, four sent him sprinting into the house in a panic. He immediately called their GP Mervyn Brigstocke, but by the time he arrived Olivia was already unconscious. She was rushed in an ambulance to Stoke Mandeville Hospital with the doctor, and Roald followed in his car.

It was too late, the little girl could not be resuscitated. She had a rare inflammation of the brain which affects one in a thousand cases of measles, and a large dose of gamma globulin could have prevented it.

This time there was nothing Roald could do to help. His precious daughter was gone, he was left 'limp with despair' and never stopped grieving. For the rest of his life Roald was unable to forgive himself for not being able to save Olivia. She was just 7-years-old.

Chapter Eleven

The shock of Olivia dying so suddenly left Roald utterly shattered. It was a searing pain from which he would never fully recover, and which haunted him until the day he died. When Theo was ill he had been able to throw himself into the practical side of his care, and working on giving his son a normal life kept him preoccupied and gave him a strong sense of purpose.

But there was nothing he could do to bring Olivia back, and Roald was struck by an overwhelming sense of anger and frustration that he had failed her in some way, that as her father he should have been able to find some way to protect his little girl. But there had been no time.

'I wish we'd had a chance to fight for her,' he told Mike Watkins simply. Nobody could console him. Theo and Tessa were still too young to understand, and he found it almost impossible to talk to Patricia who was suffering too. Patricia later told how distant her husband had become: 'He did not talk about his feelings, did not want to talk about Olivia. He wouldn't let anything come out, nothing.'

Luckily Patricia was able to find some solace in her mother-in-law – who had also endured the same pain when she had lost her eldest daughter Astri in 1920. But Roald fell silent, haunted round the clock by Olivia's death. He created an intricate Alpine garden around her grave as a living monument, and insisted on keeping all of her toys and books in his bedroom. He kept a painting of her in his hut, and framed many of her poems and paintings, but nothing could keep his demons at bay. The whole family was broken by the tragedy, but Roald simply did not have the strength to lead them through the darkness. He withdrew almost entirely from them all, isolating himself either in his writing hut or spending hours quietly tending to the garden he had created at Olivia's graveside. Unable to talk about his feelings to anyone, he attempted to numb the pain by drinking heavily every day and taking more and more of the strong barbiturates which had been prescribed for his back problems.

Olivia dying at such a young age had destroyed any last remaining shreds of belief Roald may have had in God, but as the weeks wore on he was intrigued by Patricia's firm conviction that she would see their daughter again in heaven one day; and when she suggested he might discuss his confused feelings with his old headmaster Geoffrey Fisher, Roald surprised his wife by actually agreeing. Fisher had gone on from Repton School to become Archbishop of Canterbury, and invited Roald to visit him at home in Dorset in December 1962. The former leader of the Church of England remembered his pupil with a wry fondness and understood that Roald now felt more sure than ever Christianity was a sham, but also that he was desperate to find any way out of the cloak of grief which enveloped him. Roald said:

> I wanted to ask him how he could be so absolutely sure that other creatures did not get the same special treatment as us. I sat there wondering if this great and famous churchman really knew what he was talking about and whether he knew anything at all about God or heaven, and if he didn't then who in the world did?

Sadly Fisher was unable to reassure him, and Roald left Dorset still convinced that he would have been able to keep his daughter safe if they left New York sooner and returned to Buckinghamshire, but now he feared that some sort of sinister curse was threatening him. He even considered having bad forces exorcised from the house. In a later interview with *Life* magazine he recalled those dark times, explaining:

> I was in a kind of daze. Morbid thoughts kept after me. It occurred to me that there must be some kind of tie-up and that kind of thought can run you down, you know, worrying about fate and the meaning of things.

Depression was not something middle-aged men discussed at that time, and there was almost nothing Roald could do to unravel his emotions. It was such a cold winter that his ink froze in its bottle and, overwhelmed by a sense of pointlessness and doom, he took to his bed. When he had felt similar bouts of depression creeping up on him in the past Roald had tended to dismiss it as self-indulgence and had hidden his feelings: 'The only way to cope was to bury it and not wear it on your sleeve and then roll those sleeves up and get down to putting things right,' he said.

CHAPTER ELEVEN

Tessa and Theo were confused and hurt by the way their father withdrew from them, and although Patricia was engulfed by grief too, she had no choice but to hold the family together the best she could. In her book *Waiting For Love*, Tessa wrote: 'He was beyond help. He could not speak for grief. I remember seeing his beautiful blue eyes fill with tears. I saw him weep in his bedroom, and then when he noticed me, he asked me to leave.'

Writing felt frivolous, and so Roald found some solace in charity work, volunteering to campaign for various children's organisations close to his heart, while Patricia kept herself busy with acting. He agreed that the family would join her in Los Angeles while she filmed a television series called *Ben Casey* but it only provided a temporary distraction. When they returned from the trip, Theo's seizures started again. Roald was determined that doctors should fit the valve he had helped invent and so for the ninth time in his short life Theo endured yet another operation to remove the shunt on his brain, but this time he managed to survive thirty days without a relapse and did not ever need his father's nifty little invention.

There was some much needed good news when they discovered that Patricia was pregnant again. It was enough of a boost to spur Roald back into action and he returned to the story he had started work on three years later. He had already renamed it *Charlie and the Chocolate Factory*, but now he started to really flesh out the character which would become his most memorable – Willy Wonka. The unusual sounding name came from a boomerang that Roald's brother Louis had once made for him called the Skilly Wonka. Many critics and readers have pointed out the obvious similarities between the eccentric factory owner and his creator. Wonka appeared unapproachable at first but beneath the dark surface was a spectacular magician, an adult who behaved like a child. He could be very funny but did not have any sentimentality and lived just outside of mainstream society, governed entirely by his own rules, in an imaginary world that revolved around sweets.

Both Willy and Roald had a unique ability to be seen as the type of adults with whom children could form a special friendship, since they would recognise their talents, understand their jokes and share their vulnerabilities. Both had enormous self-confidence which was often mistaken for arrogance, and preferred to keep themselves shrouded in an air of mystery. But Roald thought he was actually more like Charlie, the lonely little boy with a vivid imagination and rich sense of wonder.

Like most children, Roald had loved sweets, but his unique fascination with the production process of chocolate had started when he was a pupil at

Repton and his housemaster had agreed with the marketing department of the nearby Cadbury's factory to send each boy new chocolate bars to test. Roald absolutely loved being given the opportunity to voice his opinions, and took the job extremely seriously. He once said that a particular creation was 'too subtle for the common palate.'

As an adult he had a chocolate bar for lunch most days, and sometimes after dinner too. While working at Shell in London in his early twenties he started to make a heavy silver ball from all his sweet wrappers, a habit he continued for the rest of his life. Roald always had a giant ball of foil on his desk. When he was in America during the war he sent his mother and sisters regular supplies of chocolate which was rationed in Britain at the time, as he could not bear the idea of them going without. Even when he could afford to shop at the finest chocolatiers, Roald never lost his infectious enthusiasm for his cheap schoolboy favourites. At Gipsy House he ensured there was a constant supply of mass-market chocolate bars which he kept in a red plastic box to be produced with a cheerful flourish at the end of almost every dinner party he hosted. He would often tell the children stories he made up about the golden years between 1930 and 1937 when most of his most beloved treats were invented, including Mars, KitKat, Aero, Maltesers, Rolo and Smarties, adding that it would have been more useful for schoolchildren to learn these dates rather than the kings and queens of England, Impressionist artists or great writers.

Charlie and The Chocolate Factory was dedicated to Theo, but it was the book that saved him from despair following the death of Olivia. Roald absorbed himself in rewriting the story no less than six times, altering the narrative slightly each time, but never changing the main characters of Willy Wonka or Charlie Bucket, the kind boy who won a golden ticket to go inside the factory. The names of Charlie's fellow competition winners changed slightly during the editing process, and there had been more of them to start with, but they remained grotesque, greedy children in various forms. Some of the original children's names included Tommy Troutbeck, Miranda Grope, Marvine Prune and Herpes Trout. In an early version of the story Charlie was originally described as 'a small negro boy' who was coated in chocolate and delivered as a gift to Wonka's son Freddie. Trapped inside his shell he witnesses a robbery and, after helping to track down the thieves, Wonka rewarded him with his own sweetshop.

The Oompa Loompas who worked in the factory came later, as did the gloating songs they delivered every time a badly behaved child got their just deserts, and Charlie's Grandpa Joe was another late addition. Roald urged

Mike Watkins to forward one of his early drafts to his former editor Sheila St Lawrence because he valued her critical opinion so much. She was now living quietly in Ireland but Roald was delighted when she replied saying how much she loved it:

> I can't tell you how excited I was by the idea of the story ... It's marvellous. As soon as I got the gist of where you were going, my mind ran away with all the kinds of candy that could be brought into the story, the smells and feels and colours, and all the wonders that go into cooking and making candies.

Sheila urged him to sprinkle it with even more of his trademark humour, or what she called 'Dahlesque touches' and added: 'I hope some of my remarks will produce counter remarks in you that will stir you to flights of fancy to make the book take off and fly as it undoubtedly will.'

Her letter was exactly the sort of feedback that Roald had been waiting for and he agreed with all her fresh ideas, changes and improvements – which included one of the most iconic scenes in children's literature. At Sheila's suggestion Augustus Pottle, who later became Augustus Gloop, got stuck in a glass pipe after falling into the river of chocolate which ran through the factory.

But despite his renewed enthusiasm for the project, as months passed Roald still could not let it go. Deep down Roald believed his talents lay in writing for adults, not children, and he felt sure that Charlie Bucket was 'a boring little bugger', but of course it would be the young hero's blandness that would give him such universal appeal.

In the summer of 1962 he finally agreed to submit the fifth draft to Virginie Fowler, his editor at his American publishing company, the newly formed Random House-Knopf-Pantheon group.

Virginie knew Roald had been working on this for a long time, and she had no idea what lay in the large envelope on her desk. When he had finally sent the manuscript to his agent Mike Watkins, Roald wrote: 'If she doesn't like it then I guess we will throw it away. I do want some money out of it.'

Virginie Fowler had been given a preview of one of the most classic stories of all time, but she was not impressed and dreaded having to tell Roald that she had a number of reservations about some of the more vulgar portions of the book. She felt it was in particularly bad taste for the children to meet such gruesome ends, and pointed out that it did not fit into the usual parameters of the children's fiction genre.

As she explained in a letter to Roald: 'This world of children's books has its own set of rules, ignoring these rules does cause unnecessary difficulties for a book.' Luckily her boss Bob Bernstein, an aggressive businessman, immediately spotted the enormous potential merchandising opportunities, and sensed that they could create something very special from a financial point of view. And Alfred Knopf, head of the newly merged publishing group, agreed it was 'miraculous' and his wife pointed out it had unique appeal to children and adults alike.

As Roald tinkered with the final version of the story, Charles Marsh fell seriously ill and died in Washington, and later critics have suggested that the character Willy Wonka was actually written as a lasting tribute to Roald's garrulous, generous friend who showed so much belief in him from the start. The optimism and confidence Charles showed towards Roald was similar to the way Wonka spotted Charlie's potential in the book and gave him the factory.

When Roald had felt rejected and undervalued, an underdog like Charlie Bucket, Charles had encouraged him to keep writing, supported him financially, paying all his bills and even offering emotional therapy when his marriage was on the brink of collapse.

Remembering the wise words of advice his friend had given him, at the end of the book Wonka told Charlie: 'A grown up person won't listen to me; he won't learn. He will try to do things his own way and not mine. So I have to have a child.'

Chapter Twelve

Charlie and the Chocolate Factory made Roald a literary star. It was an instant success and critics raved about it across Europe and America. Willy Wonka was hailed as a classic Dickensian character and *The New York Times* wrote: 'Roald Dahl, a writer of spine-chilling stories for adults, proved in *James and the Giant Peach* that he knew how to appeal to children. Now he has done it again, gloriously.' The *Boston Globe* added: 'The young, with their stainless steel digestive systems, will take to it with relish.'

Roald was inundated with offers of work, and invited to join an elite group of famous writers including John Updike, Arthur Miller and Robert Graves who were each paid $2,000 to create a children's story using a very limited vocabulary. Roald thought all the other efforts were 'guaranteed to anesthetise in two minutes flat any unfortunate child who got hold of them', but he could not refuse such a large fee and in early 1963 he came up with a story about an 8-year-old girl who hated hunting. *The Magic Finger* was repeatedly turned down by Virginie Fowler, the editor at Knopf who had also picked holes in *Charlie and the Chocolate Factory*. Roald instructed Mike Watkins to take it elsewhere; and when he sold it to rival publishing house Harper for $5,000, Virginie found herself in trouble with her boss.

Alfred Knopf was already viewing Roald as his most important writer and was furious that a member of his staff had taken it upon herself to reject one of his stories without consulting him first. He fired off an angry memo saying:

> You made it clear that you thought so badly of this particular story that you felt it a great pity that it was going to be published at all, and didn't seem greatly concerned about the fact that an author closely identified with us was going to appear at least once in another imprint.
>
> I do not think a decision to refuse to publish a story by Roald Dahl should be made without discussions with, and approval

by, the very top people in Knopf and Random House. I am afraid that we are all more concerned about and embarrassed by what has happened than you realise.

After that Roald never had to deal with Virginie Fowler again.

But as the summer of 1963 wore on, it was Patricia's career that was in the spotlight once again. There had been some critical buzz around her new film *Hud*, and after both The New York Film Critics and the National Board of Review voted her best actress, it was clear that Patricia was heading for great things. At the start of 1964 she was thrilled to be nominated for an Oscar, but by the time the glittering ceremony took place that April she was eight months pregnant and decided it was not a good idea for her to fly to Los Angeles. She was convinced she had almost no chance of actually winning the award anyway, but at dawn on 13 April a phone call woke everyone in Gipsy House – Patricia had been named Best Actress for *Hud*.

Roald's former lover Annabella Power had been at the ceremony and had taken to the stage to accept the gold Academy Award statue on her friend's behalf, and as Patricia celebrated with the family over breakfast, she finally felt that her talent had received the recognition she had wanted for so many years. She said: 'Not only did my whole industry think I was good enough but now, finally, a fabulous new career was just around the corner. And we'd make a fortune.'

There was more to celebrate a few weeks later when Ophelia Magdelene Dahl was born in May, and the whole family jetted off to spend the summer in Hawaii where Patricia was filming a wartime drama *In Harm's Way*, alongside John Wayne. Although Roald did not particularly enjoy the trip – he felt the luxurious hotel which the film's director Otto Preminger had chosen for them was too ostentatious – he struck up a friendship with a budding young film director called Robert Altman who would go on to become one of the most powerful players in Hollywood. But at that time, desperate to make his name, Altman needed scripts to work with, and pleaded with Roald to write something for him.

Roald had already had a brush with the movie business, and had found it boring and slow, so only ever agreed to script writing when he needed the money.

After Theo's accident Roald had written a TV series called *Way Out* to pay the hospital bills, but he had recently launched – and won – a legal battle with MGM studios after Patricia showed him a script she had been sent with an identical plot to a story he had written years earlier.

CHAPTER TWELVE

In 1944 Roald wrote *Beware of the Dog*, about an RAF pilot who bailed out of his plane and woke up in Occupied France where English speaking Germans were determined to extract information from him. In the MGM version, called *36 Hours*, the German doctors pretended to be American, but it was similar enough for Roald to instruct Mike Watkins to complain. He told Watkins:

> This is a big matter for me. That is why I am making such a song and dance about it. It is not often in a lifetime that a storywriter has a full movie based on his story. He must, therefore get (for his children) all he possibly can out of it.

He threatened to halt production if they did not pay him at least £25,000, and after negotiating for some time, MGM eventually paid £30,000 into a trust fund account he had set up in Theo's name, and Roald told Watkins's assistant: 'If one does not fight for one's rights with these people, they will always screw you in the end.'

It left a bad taste in his mouth; Roald took very little interest in talk about a movie version of *Charlie and the Chocolate Factory*, and attempted to keep a low profile when the family headed to Los Angeles for Christmas – no easy feat when an Oscar winner touches down in town. Roald would have rather stayed at home but Patricia was filming *Seven Women* about a missionary in China who gives herself up to barbarians to save the lives of the other women, and she wanted to be with the children for Christmas. Patricia was now commanding much higher fees and the Dahls rented a sprawling mansion belonging to *Hud* director Martin Ritt. The first few days of filming required Patricia to ride a donkey for hours at a time, but she had not dared to tell the producers that she was actually three months pregnant in case they fired her. When she came home from the fourth day of filming, Roald found her doubled over in agony, complaining of a pain in her temple and double vision. Thanks to all the research he had done into neurology, Roald suspected his wife was having a stroke and called an LA based neurosurgeon he knew called Charles Carton, with whom he had been discussing bringing the Dahl-Wade-Till valve to America. Carton was alarmed and sent an ambulance for Patricia, who was by then covered in vomit and barely conscious, unable to even recognise her own highly distressed children.

Over the next few hours she suffered three major brain haemorrhages and Roald gave Carton permission to operate, fearing that Patricia probably would not survive the surgery, but there was no alternative at this stage. Doctors worked through the night, sawing a trap door into her skull to remove the clots that had formed and were spurting blood on to the surrounding brain tissue, caused by an aneurysm which could have ruptured at any time.

When Dr Carton emerged from the operating theatre in the early hours of the following morning, he warned Roald that even if Patricia did pull through, her disabilities might be so severe he could end up wishing she had not. Roald called his mother-in-law to prepare her for the worst, explaining that Patricia would be closely monitored over the next ten days to see if she regained any normal brain function, but the odds were stacked against her.

Patricia remained in a coma for three weeks, lying on an ice mattress to minimise swelling, and with anticonvulsants being dripped constantly into her system in case of another seizure, but she did not make any involuntary movements at all. Roald was constantly at her side, spending every waking hour trying to get some sort of reaction from her. He would repeat over and over again: 'Pat, this is Roald.' Sometimes he would lift her eyelids or shout in her ear: 'Tessa says hello! Theo says hello!' Once he apparently even slapped her across the face, desperate for a reaction. On February 22, *Variety* magazine ran a story with the headline: 'Film Actress Patricia Neal Dies at 39.'

From then on the hospital was besieged by photographers and fans, but Roald remained calm despite the chilling reminder of Theo's many surgeries and of course Olivia's death. Roald felt the sinister forces were out to get him again. He had been repeatedly cursed by a plague of horrific brain traumas – first his own head injuries had altered his personality in 1940, then Charles Marsh had been incapacitated by a brain inflammation, his son's skull had been shattered, another inflammation had snatched their young daughter's life, and now his wife lay in yet another hospital bed battling the aftermath of cranial surgery.

He later told journalist Barry Farrell that he was sure it was nothing more than a series of strange coincidences but at the time he felt understandably paranoid:

> Superstition is something that one grows out of. You try avoiding all the cracks in the pavement or you touch all the posts in the fence. But then you find out later that it doesn't help. You find out that it's not going to make a bit of difference if you step on the cracks or not. I think I just realise subconsciously that if you start thinking about bad luck, you're going to weaken. The great thing is to keep going, whatever happens.

The outlook was dire but Roald maintained his bedside vigil with no idea what the future held for their young family. Once again Roald was astounded by the skill of the nursing staff that cared for his wife in the early days: 'They were swift, adroit and calm,' he said. 'These girls didn't make any mistakes, and except when they were writing their reports they never sat down.'

And then quite unexpectedly on 10 March his wife – who he had started to describe as 'an enormous pink cabbage' – opened one eye. She could not move or speak and was confused, angry and scared. Astonishingly, their unborn baby had survived too. Roald was immediately optimistic at the way she had defied every medical prediction, and decided it would help Patricia's memory if she saw the children. Bringing them to her bedside was a terrible mistake; Tessa who was 7 and 4-year-old Theo were deeply disturbed by the sight of their mother who they barely recognised. Most of the hair had been shaved off her head for the surgery, she had a black patch strapped over one eye, and was covered in tubes. She was babbling but making no sense and the children were haunted for many years by what they had seen; even as an adult, Tessa said she could still sharply recall the 'horror, fear and nausea' she felt. Luckily Ophelia was too young to remember any of it.

Just as he had swung into action to save Theo when he was ill, Roald was once again a man on a mission. He was determined that he would not fail Patricia as he had failed Olivia. He was certainly not going to allow himself to be side-tracked by sympathy or emotion, which was of no practical help to Patricia. He set to work immediately, resolving to focus on what he felt was the best way to bring his wife back – and that included immediate and intense mental stimulation. He banished tearful visitors and threw out flowers and cards from well-wishers which might have distracted Patricia by encouraging her to feel sorry for herself. He hired a team of the very best speech therapists and physiotherapists to work with her round the clock. There was no let up, but Roald's ruthless approach appeared to be working, and doctors were astounded at the progress she was making just days after regaining consciousness. The speed of her recovery was truly remarkable, particularly the way she tried to put together full sentences despite remaining partially paralysed.

Roald was unwaveringly optimistic and wrote to his mother:

> In herself, she is very fit and cheerful. She smiles a great deal. She has met and completely recognised Tessa and Theo.

I think that in about four days we will get her home here to the house, with a full time living-in nurse. That will make things easier for everyone, and much pleasanter for her. They are going to put a steel brace on her right leg to help her to walk. The children are all fine, and everyone is very braced by Pat's condition.

Miraculously, just a month after she had suffered the massive stroke which very nearly killed her, Patricia was discharged. There was a huge pack of reporters and photographers waiting to catch a glimpse of her leaving hospital. She wore a headscarf to cover the scars on her shaved head, and still needed the eye patch, but as Roald pushed his wife in a wheelchair he remarked cheerfully: 'Her thought processes are perfect, she is a tremendous fighter!'

She was far from being well enough to fly back to England, so Roald took Patricia to recover back at the Ritt's mansion which they were now borrowing rent-free in Pacific Palisades. She was inundated with well-wishers, even Frank Sinatra sent a gramophone player and a stack of records, but Roald made it abundantly clear that visitors were not welcome; Patricia was vulnerable and he was determined to protect her at any cost. She was physically exhausted and mentally overwhelmed when she started to fully understand the extent of the capabilities she had lost. Patricia was floored by the sheer impossibility that life would ever be the same again.

Despite Roald's encouragement, the nurses and physiotherapists found their patient disinterested and difficult to work with, and privately he was forced to admit that they had a long and difficult task ahead: 'If left alone, she would sit and stare into space and in half an hour a great black cloud of depression would envelop her mind,' he said. 'Unless I was prepared to have a bad-tempered desperately unhappy nitwit in the house, some very drastic action would have to be taken.'

The drastic action meant increasing Patricia's speech therapist from one hour a day to four or sometimes five. It was far more than she could manage, and experts warned Roald that continuing to push Patricia so hard could be harmful in the long term, but he thought it was more dangerous for her to be idle. He was also beginning to suspect that she was actually stronger than she appeared, and was concealing some of her progress in the hope that he would relax a little. Roald suspicions were confirmed when the director Mel Brooks and his actress wife Anne Bancroft, who had taken over Patricia's role in *Seven Women*, invited the Dahls for dinner and Patricia accepted enthusiastically. They expected her to arrive in a wheelchair, if she could even make it to their house at all, but were astounded to see her walking unaided from the car, although she seemed to have trouble following the conversation.

While doctors generally accepted the evidence that Roald's gruelling, almost military style regime was instrumental in Patricia's rapid recovery, others feared he was far too strict and completely lacking in any human compassion or warmth. Patricia's mother Eura was particularly distressed and complained to Roald's sister Else that she was being excluded; and Else was forced to explain that her brother's detached attitude may seem strange from the outside but he had gone into 'survival mode'.

He would not risk losing another loved one. Else explained: 'Any strong emotional element was likely to be damaging. They have been through so much together that it has strengthened their love and trust of each other.'

The US medical bills were mounting up rapidly and as soon as Patricia was declared fit for travel, Roald insisted on returning to England, where they would be surrounded by family and he could at least try to work again. Their friend Cary Grant drove them to the airport, where Patricia gave a fifteen-minute press conference before walking unaided on to the plane. Roald announced that he was no longer relying on any medical advice and her astonishingly successful recovery plan was entirely down to him: 'I called in no doctors,' he told reporters. 'It was a matter that had to be sorted out by the family alone.'

Chapter Thirteen

Back in Buckinghamshire, Patricia dreaded being left alone with Roald who said he intended to focus on nothing but her recovery without distraction, but the house was teeming with staff, including a nurse, speech therapists, physiotherapists, a nanny for the children and housekeepers. His strict strategy for Patricia's rehabilitation was that she must be kept busy to avoid boredom, frustration or depression setting in. Fearing at first that she might be suicidal, he dispatched her to a nearby RAF military hospital for boot-camp style physiotherapy but she hated it and insisted on being treated at home.

When friends heard that she was back they wanted to visit but were made to feel decidedly unwelcome by Roald, who insisted his wife should not receive special treatment, and rejected most offers of help unless they wanted to come and keep Patricia's mind active with specific memory games, maths and puzzles.

Roald encouraged various elderly neighbours with time on their hands to spend time reading to her and urged them to be as firm as he was, but many of these amateur tutors found Roald abrupt and the atmosphere uncomfortable. Patricia found it deeply humiliating to have help with very basic tasks, and the sessions often ended in tears. Tessa wrote later:

> She would shout and scream. Make up words that we didn't understand and then laugh hysterically. Every day swarms of visitors would come and sit with her. On my father's instructions they would make her study, like a kindergarten child, reading, writing and arithmetic. Theo was more advanced at school than she was.

Anne Bancroft insisted on paying for professional nurses to fly over from Los Angeles, but they too found Patricia angry or unintelligible. Roald was convinced that constant stimulation was the key and he eventually found someone who agreed with him. A woman called Valerie Eaton Griffith, a former beauty therapist in her early forties, had come to live in the village to be with her elderly father and heard that her neighbours needed help. The first moment she met Patricia she realised this once confident woman had lost her self esteem and set about tailoring Roald's strategy to focus on the activities which had a positive effect on her mental health, and cutting down on those which made her feel frustrated, angry or humiliated.

Roald was enormously impressed with Valerie's business like efficiency and was delighted to take a step back, soon handing over nearly all Patricia's care so he could get back to work. It helped of course that Patricia liked her too, and they were soon working together two or three times a week for up to six hours at a time. By making himself an expert on stroke recovery strategies, Roald had saved his wife, and ended up writing a popular and practical self-help guide called *A Stroke In The Family*. Years later when he was invited to speak at the Speech Rehabilitation Institute, he said:

> I was often criticised at the time for pushing the patient too hard, but when you're talking about real life as opposed to vegetable life, you're in a crisis and you don't stop to enquire whether the patient is comfortable or not. Nothing was smooth or easy. In fact at one time I took her to a psychiatrist to make sure she didn't intend to carry out her threats of suicide.

Although he did everything in his power to regain some sense of normality, life would never be the same for Mr and Mrs Dahl. Patricia had changed beyond all recognition since the aneurysm and she knew it. The cracks in their rocky relationship had been papered over in the past by the children, and patched up when they endured the tragic loss of their daughter and their son's terrible accidents together; but now Patricia knew that the calamity they faced was her. She was the burden. She was no longer the glamorous young movie star he had married, she had lost all her power and instead felt dependent on her husband, like another one of his children. She found his endless updates and calculations about her progress particularly irritating:

> He would tell me I was 42 per cent better than yesterday and 51 per cent better than last week. God I was so sick of his percentages, his plans, his programs, his world. It was Papa's world now. He was a hero and I was hating him.

She had no choice but to give her care up to Roald and on 4 August 1965, Patricia gave birth to the baby who had defied death and survived her mother's stroke. It was a miracle nobody had been sure they would see, but Patricia was photographed just hours after delivering another daughter, Lucy Neal Dahl, drinking beer and playing dominoes.

Just days later Roald gave an upbeat interview predicting that she would soon be ready to make a triumphant return to acting and continue with a number of eagerly awaited films that had been put on hold since her stroke: 'Pat realizes she must rise to the challenge I have set for her and she is doing it,' he said. But behind the scenes, his wife shared none of his optimism since she could not yet walk properly and had not even dared to glance at a script. When she attempted to memorise lines of poetry they came out as confused jumbled words of nonsense. But Roald never let up, and would not allow her even a moment of self-pity, and as a result of his confidence, major movie roles began to trickle in again.

Director Mike Nichols offered her the part of notorious seductress Mrs Robinson opposite Dustin Hoffman in *The Graduate* but Patricia did not feel confident that she was ready to do the role justice, and the part famously went to her good friend Anne Bancroft instead. The comedy actor Peter Sellers urged Patricia to make a cameo appearance in his film *What's New Pussycat?* but she turned that down too. She finally plucked up the courage to accept an offer from Angela Lansbury's brother Edgar who wanted her in the lead role in a film adaptation of the play *The Subject Was Roses*. She would play a tough New York mother whose son, played by Martin Sheen, would return home from the Second World War to find his parents' marriage was failing. Filming would be taking place mostly in Manhattan in the Spring of 1967, although Patricia was anxious that she was returning to work too soon; she felt unattractive and dreaded the harsh glare of the spotlight being turned on her again. But Valerie Eaton Griffith was doing wonders for her self-confidence, and had already somehow managed to persuade her to fly to New York anyway to deliver a speech at a celebrity dinner in her honour in March 1967. With her husband proudly on her arm, she made it to the star-studded gala, An Evening With Patricia Neal, where guests including Paul Newman, Leonard Bernstein, Rock Hudson and Joan Crawford gave her a standing ovation for the speech which Roald had written. The evening raised more than $90,000 for brain injured children; and it was just the tonic Patricia needed. She publicly made a point of thanking her husband for successfully convincing her that she was ready to step back into the public eye. She knew that she could not have done it without Roald pushing her every step of the way: 'I knew at that moment that Roald the slave driver, Roald the bastard, with his relentless courage, Roald the Rotten, as I had called him more than once, had thrown me back into the deep water. Where I belonged,' she said later.

She arrived on set for the first day of filming feeling positive for the first time since the stroke, but when it began to dawn on Patricia what an enormous task lay ahead, including memorising a five-page monologue, her confidence quickly evaporated. She was finding it almost impossible to learn her lines and in a revealing interview with *New York Post* journalist Cindy Adams, she let slip that Roald had actually pushed her into making the commitment before she was ready: 'It is not my desire to work at all. My husband coerced me. He felt that my rehabilitation would only be completed once I was back at work,' she said. 'I'm no longer used to the hustle and bustle and rushing and fittings and make up tests and press interviews.'

There were a few wobbles along the way but Patricia made it all the way through filming with Roald and Valerie by her side, and when the film was released in 1968 her performance won glowing reviews. A critic from *New York* magazine said he was 'left groping for superlatives', while another said: 'She no longer indicates suffering, she defines it.'

The role led to another Oscar nomination, and Patricia had not just been reborn, she had risen from the dead – and Roald's tough approach was widely credited as the key. In a blaze of publicity surrounding her comeback Roald admitted he had been cruel to be kind, taking much of the credit for convincing her to take the role: 'Pat's not ambitious,' he said. 'I really did have to bully her into making another film. She didn't want to do it.'

Privately they both refused to admit that Patricia had changed and not for the better. She was no longer affectionate with Roald, on the contrary she was vindictive and obsessive, although he convinced himself these personality defects were temporary, they were just another part of her recovery and he remained optimistic that she would return to her old self, given the progress she had made in only six months.

As well as confiding in Valerie, Roald found another unlikely source of support in the young journalist Barry Farrell who was invited to live with the family for an in-depth article he was writing for *Life* magazine which would later be expanded to a unique account of her recovery in his book called *Pat and Roald*. Roald could be utterly charming if he wanted to be, and Barry was immediately bowled over by his infectious optimism when it came to Patricia's health, although he later expressed concerns that such a harsh approach could ever be a complete success. Far from resenting the intrusion of Farrell's near constant presence, Roald enjoyed having an ally among a sea of women, and struck up a close rapport with the 30-year-old writer who slotted into life at Gipsy House so well that he was even invited to join the Dahls on their family holiday. The pair took long walks together and Barry described him as 'the best storyteller I know,' adding 'listening to him often worked a kind of spell on me.'

Although Roald occasionally complained to Mike Watkins behind Barry's back about the 'endless talks and probings', he did not ask him to leave as he had calculated that the article and ensuing book could lead to £100,000 worth of publicity. There was already talk about film rights too. But when he read the final manuscript in 1968 Roald was horrified by the way Barry described Patricia's personality. He said she had changed dramatically in the aftermath of the stroke, becoming intolerant and unpredictable, self-centred and demanding, and was probably an alcoholic. He told how she obsessively picked up litter and complained about lights being left on. Although Roald may have privately admitted there was some truth in the account if he were being honest with himself, he went straight to Barry's publishers accusing him of libel and threatening to block publication unless they made the changes he wanted. He pointed out that Farrell was in no position to judge any differences in Patricia's personality since he had not known her before her stroke, and insisted very firmly on the removal of the suggestion that the children's nanny Sheena Burt had slapped Patricia over her mistreatment of Ophelia. Patricia was equally wounded and wrote directly to Barry, whom she had welcomed into her home, complaining that he had portrayed her as 'the bitchy woman'. She added: 'I am not a drunk! I am not a drunk! I am not a drunk! At least I don't think so!' Barry agreed to make the changes they demanded prior to publication, but was upset that the couple had been so hurt by what he saw as an accurate and unique insight into their fascinating marriage. He replied to them:

> It was not a cruel book … A great deal was left out to protect your feelings and your privacy. Nonetheless, you attacked it using means that suggested contempt for the work as well as for the friendship of the author. I feel stung and betrayed by you and I regret every day that I ever gave an hour to writing the vain, false book that is now to be issued under my name.

Some time later Roald invited Barry over to discuss the matter, but he refused to ever speak to them again, even when his book was made into a television film in 1981 starring Glenda Jackson as Patricia and Dirk Bogarde playing Roald. Since Bogarde was a neighbour at the time, Roald offered the actor a unique insight into how to portray him: 'I do not display emotions,' he advised. 'They may churn madly inside, but I always keep them there. Unsentimental. I am cool and competent in a crisis. Act swiftly, never get visibly excited.' He added: 'The act of rehabilitating Pat was like writing a long and difficult novel.'

The film focused on the remarkable way in which Roald had dealt with the aftermath of the crisis and pushed his wife almost beyond her limits, both physically and emotionally. The happy ending to the film left viewers with the distinct impression that Patricia's recovery was pretty much complete and that the famous family was as strong and tight-knit as ever. In reality that was far from the case.

Their daughter Tessa was unhappy at home, she could not stand the arguments and begged her parents to send her away to boarding school. Although Roald had managed to transform Patricia from someone who could only communicate in meaningless grunts into an Oscar nominee in less than three years, she was no longer the wild and bewitching woman who had been 'tamed' by Roald. Her friend, actress Maria Tucci, said she was more like 'an adorable but rather odd 10-year-old'. Patricia still limped and was frustrated by gaps in her memory. Roald no longer felt physical desire for his wife who seemed more like a dependent child than his lover. She loudly complained that sex was 'agony' and as their marriage began to collapse under the strain, they could no longer conceal their differences.

Although she would win a Golden Globe Award for her performance in *The Homecoming* in 1972, toward the end of the Sixties the pressure was on Roald to support the family whose medical bills and school fees were mounting up.

Against his better judgement, he felt he was left with no option but to plunge himself back into the world of movie making. Since meeting Robert Altman in Hawaii he had been half-heartedly working on a script for him about RAF pilots with the title *Oh Death, Where Is Thy Sting-a-ling-aling?* They had agreed that Roald would only be paid when Altman sold the project to a studio, which was no easy task since he had not yet directed his own film.

Roald had successfully convinced his friend Cary Grant to take an interest in playing the lead role but he also doubted Altman's abilities, and Mike Watkins warned Roald that he was being far too trusting of this young television director he barely knew. However, by April 1965 there was a generous $150,000 offer on the table from United Artists – but they would not let Altman direct it. Roald wanted his share of the money for Patricia's nurses, physiotherapists and speech therapy, so urged Altman to take the offer and allow someone else to take the reins. Altman refused, meaning Roald was left with nothing, and the two men had a bitter fall out. Six weeks later however, Hollywood agent Irving 'Swifty' Lazar persuaded Altman to change his mind and they split the proceeds down the middle. After paying Lazar ten per cent, Roald had $67,500 to put into a trust fund for Theo and Tessa, but he never forgave Altman and they never really patched up their friendship.

But Roald could hardly complain since he was then paid another $25,000 on top for rewriting his script for the film's new director David Miller. Roald dismissed Miller as being 'extraordinarily ignorant'; the film was a flop at the box office, but his script was good enough to get him noticed by two other United Artist producers – Harry Saltzman and Albert 'Cubby' Broccoli, who owned the James Bond film franchise. Suddenly Roald realised he was in the running to write the screen adaptation of his old friend Ian Fleming's 007 novel *You Only Live Twice*. He and Fleming had hit it off many years earlier when they both worked in William Stephenson's shadowy espionage operations in America during the war, and had admired each other's remarkably similar attitudes towards drinking, gambling and womanising. Roald said Fleming was: 'A sparky, witty, caustic companion, full of jokes and also full of odd obscure bits of knowledge.' In Roald's opinion, *You Only Live Twice* was his worst book, and he warned the producers that he would need to make some major changes to the storyline. They said he could do whatever he liked as long as he did not alter the famous 'girl formula'. With that, Roald let his imagination run wild, dreaming up many of the movie's most famous scenes including a battle between miniature helicopters and a spacecraft that swallowed another. The script took him just eight weeks to write; the producers were thrilled, and filming started with Sean Connery almost immediately. Although Roald told Mike Watkins it was 'the biggest load of bullshit I've ever put my hand to', he had hit the jackpot financially. Roald was paid $165,000 and treated himself to a chauffeur driven Rolls Royce, boasting to friends that he had made so much money that he never needed to work again. But then Cubby Broccoli suggested he adapt another of Fleming's books: *Chitty Chitty Bang Bang*.

Chapter Fourteen

Roald did not think much of *Chitty Chitty Bang Bang*. In his considered opinion the story of a madcap inventor who creates a flying car was 'simple, rather childish', but when he was offered $125,000 with a percentage of the film's profits on top, along with a generous agreement to have his fee paid into an offshore account to avoid paying UK income tax, Roald was hardly in any position to refuse. He said he was only doing it so there would be enough money left for the children if he died, and hoped that Patricia would soon be well enough to return to work; once he started work however, Roald found himself enjoying the project. He peppered the script with a number of typically Dahlesque touches including the toot sweets, candy whistles which summoned all the dogs in the neighbourhood, and the sinister Child Catcher who lured children into his cage with sweets. Like so many of his other grotesque characters, including Willy Wonka, Aunts Spiker and Sponge, and later Miss Trunchbull in *Matilda*, the Child Catcher trod a masterful line between evil and comic.

Chitty Chitty Bang Bang was a global smash hit which remains an enduring classic even today, and Roald seemed to be revelling in his new-found celebrity status and the great wealth it brought, although he often protested loudly and publicly about how much he loathed everything about the film industry. He was gaining a reputation for being somewhat unpredictable and tactless, which may have been the reason he did not receive an invitation to the film's charity premiere where he would have had a chance to meet the queen. After discovering he had been left off the VIP guest list, Roald told friends he was furious about the snub. Despite the success of *You Only Live Twice* and *Chitty Chitty Bang Bang*, Roald felt he was being deliberately excluded from the high profile event by Cubby and complained to his old friend Swifty Lazar:

> I am sure you are aware that I personally don't give a damn whether we met the Royal Family or not. What I did care about

was Cubby's behaviour and the way I have been treated all through. I have now produced two worthwhile original scripts for Cubby and as far as I can tell, have done nothing wrong. It makes me cross.

He was offered several more screenwriting opportunities, including an adaptation of Aldous Huxley's novel *Brave New World*, and Ludovic Kennedy's *10 Rillington Place*, about serial killer John Christie, but turned them down saying he was tired of films and wanted to get back to writing his own children's stories.

He certainly had no interest in real-life crime stories because he found them sordid, humourless and said they had no entertainment value. He said: 'A macabre story, if it shall be successful, must have a quality about it that makes one smile at the same time that it makes one wriggle. That is the secret.'

What he wanted was a project for Patricia to get her teeth into; he was keen for her to return to work, and so he agreed to adapt a psychological thriller called *Nest in a Falling Tree* about a spinster called Maura Prince who falls in love with a mysterious handyman without realising he is a rapist and murderer. In his new script Roald made Maura a recovering stroke victim with Patricia in mind for the role, and renamed it *The Night Digger*, but no matter how hard he tried to make it work, his heart was simply not in it. Since Roald owned the rights to the story, it fell to him to negotiate a production deal with a film studio, but he could not stand the slow-moving process, he loathed having to hash out the fine print of contracts, and was deeply frustrated whenever he had to attend endless meetings which never seemed to reach a satisfactory conclusion.

He eventually managed to strike a deal with Youngstreet Productions and a director called Alastair Reid, agreeing that he would not take a fee upfront, but would get a significant share of the profits after the film was released. When filming got underway, Patricia made it clear that her husband was not welcome on the set; she felt he undermined her confidence so much with his observations on her acting skills that she vowed she would never make another movie again.

'I don't really care about making films now,' she said afterwards. 'I was so ambitious once. But I don't really want to work. I would not care a lot if I don't do another film. I am just pleased I am married to the man who is my husband.' After Patricia told Roald that she would rather do without his feedback, he avoided going on set whenever possible. He hated travelling anyway and was relieved to no longer feel obliged to make arduous journeys to the various filming locations, so he was content to sit back and let Alistair Reid get on with it. Roald only bothered to watch a rough cut when filming was almost complete, and was shocked by how many major changes Reid had made to the script. He was appalled by the amount of gratuitous sex scenes that had been added, but by then it was too late to alter anything: 'It was unbelievable. All Pat's big scenes had been cut and the entire film was a mess of pornographic junk with men and women copulating all over the place. We were aghast,' Roald said. The film flopped in America and was never released in Britain, so Roald never made any money from it, and admitted defeat.

By now he was a millionaire and no longer needed the money on offer as a scriptwriter as the children's trust funds were bulging and the entire family would be very well taken care of after his death. He had accepted that the film industry was not for him, and the market for short stories seemed to be drying up too. His most recent short stories for adults *The Visitor* and *The Last Act* had been rejected, and he decided to return the $100 a year that *The New Yorker* magazine was still paying him to have the first look at all his stories. And so, after a five-year break, he returned to children's fiction.

He was forced to agree that this was where his real talents lay – *Charlie and the Chocolate Factory* had sold more than 600,000 copies in America, and sales of *James and the Giant Peach* topped 250,000, earning him almost $1m in royalties. Roald decided to redouble his efforts to get both the books published in Britain. It seems impossible to imagine now, but it took him seven years to achieve this since they were rejected by at least eleven major publishing houses. By the end of 1964 he was ready to give up and told Mike Watkins: 'I refuse to peddle these two nice children's books all over London at random, to get one rejection after another. Merely to flog the books round indiscriminately until they have been rejected by all of London is absurd.'

But as luck would have it, Tessa lent a copy of *James and the Giant Peach* to her school friend Camilla Unwin, the daughter of Rayner Unwin, who had recommended J. R. R. Tolkein's classic children's tale *The Hobbit* to his own father Sir Stanley Unwin. Sir Stanley was the head of the publishing house George Allen & Unwin. When Rayner noticed his daughter so completely engrossed in the book he was surprised he had not heard of it; which is when he realised it had not yet been published in Britain, and immediately seized the opportunity for himself.

He contacted Roald at once and they arranged a meeting to hash out a deal. The agreement the two men finally made was unusual because it would see Roald earning nothing at all until Unwin had recouped all their initial printing costs. After that Roald would receive fifty per cent of all the future sales – it was a gamble because if the books were not popular Roald would not see a penny. But usually authors only got ten or twenty per cent of each copy sold, and Roald was a keen gambler. No other publishers were interested anyway, and so they sealed the agreement.

Of course it more than paid off. Within weeks of both books being published in 1967 they had completely sold out. They were reprinted over and over again, and the publishers had trouble keeping up with the demand from bookshops up and down the county. When Unwin published *The Magic Finger* the following year, that flew off the shelves too. Readers were clamouring for more, so Roald sat down to flesh out another idea he had about a cunning fox who leads his starving family away from the sights of three evil farmers, Boggis, Bunce and Bean.

The Fantastic Fox looked set to be another triumph but the final version was not quite as Roald had wanted it. In his initial draft Mr Fox would end up victorious when he dug a tunnel into a supermarket and his family helped themselves to food, but his American publishers at Random House were concerned. They did not want to be seen as glorifying theft and felt uncomfortable about the way the conflict between the animals and the trio of farmers could be easily compared to human military warfare at a time when many American citizens were protesting against the recent US involvement in the Vietnam War.

In the early version, Mr Fox told his family:

> They have declared war on us. And in a war there is no such thing as stealing. When one country is fighting another country, as they always seem to be doing up there, does the general say to his soldiers, 'You mustn't steal from the enemy?' They do worse than steal. They bomb and blast and kill and do everything they possibly can to destroy what the enemy has.

The president and CEO of Random House Bob Bernstein was a big fan of Roald's work. His stories had made him a very rich man, but he also knew that Roald never took criticism well. Bob would need to tread very carefully when it came to raising these sensitive matters with his star author. Bob had been warned that Roald had already been threatening to take his work to rival publishers if he felt underappreciated by Random House, and that would mean risking a massive drop in profits. It took Bernstein almost a month to work out exactly what to say so Roald to avoid upsetting him, and even when he did eventually suggest a number of changes to the scenes involving stealing, he was conciliatory, pre-empting Roald's displeasure. Bob said: 'If we can't convince you to change, in the end we will do it your way.'

As predicted, Roald fought back against the changes, arguing: 'Foxes live by stealing.' He also pointed out that had Beatrix Potter worried about animals taking food that was not theirs, then half of her classic children's stories would never have been published.

They were stuck in a deadlock over the issue for four months. Nobody was quite sure what to do, and so nobody did anything. Neither side seemed prepared to back down and the manuscript lay untouched with no publication date in sight, until an editor called Fabio Coen found it on his desk. Coen loved the story and proposed a clever way of keeping both Roald and his bosses happy. Best of all, the solution he came up with did not involve too much rewriting of the original story. He suggested that the foxes should still be allowed to steal food as Roald wanted, but they should raid the farmyards of their tormentors rather than the supermarket, which would remove any accusations of shoplifting.

Roald was thrilled with Coen's smart way of solving the issue and wrote him a letter glowing with praise, telling him:

> You have come up with suggestions so good that I almost feel as though I am committing plagiarism in accepting them. So I won't accept them. I'll grab them with both hands. No editor with whom I have ever dealt has ever before produced such a constructive and sensible idea.

Roald also agreed to change the name from *The Fantastic Fox* to *Fantastic Mr Fox*, and when the book was eventually published at the end of 1970 it became another instant bestseller.

Roald dedicated it to the memory of Olivia, and told friends that while he still thought about his daughter constantly, perhaps the pain was a little less raw and the scars were at least beginning to heal. He started to reflect on other aspects of his life too. He had achieved a great deal and was rapidly becoming a household name. Financially he was secure and no longer needed to take on dreaded movie scripts. Both his wife and son were in good heath and the outlook for both of them had already far exceeded what any doctors could have possibly predicted. Although he did not have particularly expensive taste, Roald decided he could afford to spend some of his money. He had always enjoyed art dealing and so decided to buy a vacant shop in Great Missenden to buy and sell antiques. He also treated himself to a number of quite valuable paintings, including four by the painter Francis Bacon. He set about stocking his cellar with a large collection of good quality Bordeaux and Burgundy wine, and installed a swimming pool in the garden of Gipsy House to the delight of his children and their friends. The Dahls operated something of an open-door policy at Gipsy House, with friends and neighbours always welcome to drop by for a dip in the pool, or for Roald to sign their copies of his books. Wildly unconventional compared to other husbands and fathers, Roald was especially popular with local children since he was always at home while their dads were at work, joining them for lunch or collecting them from school. Many who knew Roald then likened him to Mr Fox, creating fun and frolics for his family in the face of any adversity.

But Patricia was not in thrall to her enterprising husband like Mrs Fox was; she never had been, and now she had become even more difficult and demanding, Roald felt like he was being driven away. The tension between them was building up but both were afraid to sit down and openly air their grievances in case daring to say it out loud brought the whole marriage crashing down around them. Patricia was only too painfully aware that her glittering jet-set lifestyle lay far behind them. While her star status was fading and she was feeling less feminine than ever, her tall and handsome husband, who had slept with some of the most beautiful, exciting and exotic women in the world, had not lost his insatiable sexual appetite.

Roald had enjoyed a string of brief and meaningless flings, but his lovers were often older than him and usually married. When the women in question were in the public eye and not wanting to risk a scandal he usually found the romance fizzled out fast. He was linked to the cosmetics guru Elizabeth Arden, who was forty years his senior, and the Marchioness of Huntly, Pamela Berry. Although she was married, he and Pamela saw each other often between 1948 and 1952, with Roald travelling to Jamaica, Scotland, Scandinavia and Wales to meet with her. Seemingly untroubled by guilt, Roald described Pamela's husband as 'a small mousy ex second hand car dealer', although her daughter later remembered Roald as 'a lovely man.'

CHAPTER FOURTEEN

But since her stroke Patricia was not the woman she once was and Roald would occasionally make digs about their dwindling sex life, joking to Patricia that she was getting too old for him, and there were various occasions when she doubted his fidelity. She never forgot a remark he made when she was expecting Lucy: 'When you go into hospital to have the baby, I think I'll go into London and find myself a girl. Someone not quite so fossilized,' he said.

Roald privately feared his marriage was doomed but there was no question of him walking out on Patricia when she needed him more than ever, and he could not bear the idea of his children being angry with him, or for them to feel abandoned.

By the start of the Seventies, his chronic back pain was worse than ever and he needed a series of major operations. While he was in hospital, to add to his misery, his mother Sofie Magdalene passed away on the fifth anniversary of Olivia's death. He was in too much agony to even attend her funeral; without her support and guidance he felt broken and weak. Her lack of sentimentality had always helped him feel tough, but he was in such pain and so focused on his own survival that he could barely mourn her passing. He realised he was dreading going home from the hospital, knowing he did not have the strength in him to hold the family together, and Patricia was not equipped to provide her husband with the support he needed. She threw regular tantrums and even her daughter Tessa described her as 'helpless, hard to live with and very self involved'.

When Patricia came to visit Roald at the hospital with a bunch of grapes to cheer him up he hurled them out of the window. He was tired of her.

Chapter Fifteen

The Dahl household was generally a calmer place when Patricia was away, and in the early 1970s she and Roald agreed she was well enough to seriously consider a number of small job offers which had been coming her way. In 1972 she was making a television commercial for Maxim's coffee, and the production company dispatched a stylist to Gipsy House to discuss her wardrobe for the shoot. Nobody could have known that it would be the final straw for Roald and Patricia's crumbling marriage.

Felicity Crossland, known as Liccy, was 33-years-old and stunningly beautiful, with striking dark hair and a complexion inherited from her father, an Indian doctor. Her mother, Elizabeth Throckmorton, was an aristocratic descendent of a lady-in-waiting to Elizabeth I who had married Sir Walter Raleigh. Liccy had married young and had three children by the age of 25, but following her divorce she was supporting herself and daughters Neisha, Charlotte and Lorina by working in commercials. Her charm and elegance made her hugely popular in the television industry, and she was the obvious choice when it came to making 'difficult' stars feel special. When the commercial director Adrian Lyne cast Patricia he knew she had a reputation for diva-type behaviour and he warned Liccy to tread carefully in Buckinghamshire that morning.

When she arrived, Liccy was met by Patricia who was already drinking a Bloody Mary at eleven o'clock in the morning, but both women had jobs to do and cheerfully discussed clothes and different looks for the shoot until Roald arrived for lunch an hour later. Roald by now was 56 and walking with difficulty after his various spinal procedures, he felt worn down and world-weary. But the moment he laid eyes on Liccy in his house that day, everything changed. He fell in love at first sight for the first time in his life. They did not exchange a word, but Liccy felt it too. The atmosphere in the room crackled with tension, and afterwards Liccy admitted it was 'electric'.

CHAPTER FIFTEEN

Roald had never experienced anything like it and realised to his horror that he had never actually fallen in love before. Patricia had no idea what was going on right under her eyes. The night before shooting on the commercial began Liccy had to visit Patricia at her hotel in London to drop off the clothes she had selected. After the fitting Roald offered to help Liccy carry her bags. Nervous, flustered and trying to be polite she pretended she had read his book but got the title the wrong way round and called it 'Someone You Like'. Roald thought she was adorable and did not correct her mistake as he usually would have done, but instead invited her to join them for dinner that evening. Fearing that might be seen as unprofessional, Liccy refused but Roald could not get her out of his mind. A few weeks later he asked her again, piling on the pressure this time, urging her to accept because his famous friend Francis Bacon needed a lift. She knew he was trying to impress her and was flattered, but her filming commitments meant Liccy had to cancel at the last minute. To make amends she invited Roald and Patricia for dinner at her flat in Battersea, south London, and pulled out all the stops to impress them too. In a bid to break the tension she also invited film director Ridley Scott, her father, and the actor Hugh Hudson the same evening. The chemistry between them was so blatant that during the meal Roald actually leant over and asked his wife for permission to have dinner with Liccy when she was away.

Patricia realised what was going on and there was not a thing she could do about it. She knew she was powerless to stand in their way, and said later: 'She wanted him and knew how to get him.' Roald was besotted and urged his close friend Annabella Power, who had long been aware of his marital problems, to help with his romantic pursuit. She was sympathetic and when Roald discovered that Liccy was travelling to Paris a few weeks later for filming with Hugh Hudson he asked if she would mind collecting an umbrella from Annabella who lived in the French capital. When Liccy arrived at the chic apartment, Annabella explained that Roald had poured out his intimate feelings in an emotional letter to her which he wanted her to share. 'He cannot stop thinking about you,' Annabella explained. 'He's madly in love with you. He thinks you are the most wonderful person in the world.'

Of course there was no umbrella but under the same pretext, Roald and Liccy arranged to meet when she returned to London. Roald took Liccy for dinner at the exclusive and discreet Curzon House Club in Mayfair, and afterwards they kissed for the first time in his car. Roald's fate was sealed at that moment. The kiss was the start of a ten-year affair that would ultimately destroy what was left of his doomed marriage to Patricia.

Since Liccy had only recently finalised her long and bitter divorce, she made it quite clear that she had absolutely no interest in marrying Roald, and was happy to keep their adultery completely secret. Of course he agreed, a fling suited him perfectly too, as he felt so responsible for Patricia's care and feared she would be lost without him. And so in 1974 Roald and Liccy began a pattern of regular trysts: whenever he could find an excuse to get away he would carefully select a bottle of wine from his cellar and buy two Dover sole from the fishmonger in the village, before driving the fifty minutes to her South London flat for dinner. But as the months passed their liaisons developed beyond their physical connection as they discovered how much they had in common. Roald had finally met a woman who genuinely shared his great passions for antiques, art, good food and fine wine. Liccy was not only beautiful, funny and intelligent, she was strong and independent and he loved that fact the she did not need – or want – looking after.

On top of all that, the icing on the cake came when they worked out that she had been born just a few streets away from his own birthplace in Llandaff, Roald felt destiny had meant to draw them together and he was completely smitten.

In one of his many passionate love letters to Liccy he wrote: 'My Darling, for nearly a year and a half I have been seeing you fairly often. But with each month and each week that goes by, the desire to see you more and more often grows stronger and stronger. It has become absolutely necessary that I see you and touch you and talk to you every few days, and I suppose that's what real love is all about. Lovemaking is another department, and of course that is also necessary. But the prime necessity, the first longing, the thing that has become vital and essential is 'contact', meeting together in a room, sitting down and talking, allowing the warmth to pass from one to another, the marvellous gentle warmth of love.'

Although she had her suspicions, Roald assured Patricia that he and Liccy were simply good friends, and she soon became a regular visitor, often joining them for dinner and even occasionally on family holidays. Liccy, who shared Roald's love of gambling, was frequently invited for nights out with him and Patricia at his favourite casino in Mayfair, the Curzon House Club, which held fond memories as it had also been the setting for their first date.

As the affair became more intense, the two families seemed to bond together. It helped that Liccy's three daughters got on well with the Dahl children, who noticed that their father became more warm and tactile with them with them whenever Liccy was around. Tessa, Ophelia, Theo and Lucy all adored Liccy from the start, she was young, bright and fun, and dazzled them straight away.

But they were careful not to flaunt their relationship too openly, and managed to keep it quiet for years. Roald would drive to the phone box in the village whenever he wanted to ring Liccy, and she rarely called him at home either. After a while he bought his own flat close to hers in Battersea, telling Patricia it would be a useful investment as the children could use it when they were older and left home, and he would be more comfortable sleeping there than in hotel beds when he needed to stay in town – which he did whenever Patricia was away working and the children were at boarding school.

But their secret was eventually discovered by Tessa who hated her first boarding school Rodean, and was moved to Downe House in Kent, but had trouble settling there too, and walked out at the age of 16. Having abandoned formal education, she announced that she had decided to move back home and help her father care for Patricia. Of course, that would have been the last thing Roald wanted at the time, and perhaps sensing how unwelcome she was Tessa began to behave erratically. Tessa had long felt as if she was competing for her father's attention with a ghost; convinced Olivia was his favourite child even though she had been dead for years. Tessa became increasingly demanding and neurotic, to such an extreme extent that Roald once admitted he was actually frightened of his daughter and found it difficult to calm her down. Some time later Tessa later claimed that Roald would medicate her with barbiturates, which he told her were 'wonderful sleeping pills'.

One night when Patricia was away and Roald did not think he needed to make his usual trip to the telephone box, Tessa overheard him whispering on the phone to Liccy in Paris and revealed: 'I think he just presumed he'd drugged me sufficiently not to hear. But I heard him have this phenomenally amorous conversation, which was nothing like I'd heard him have with anyone else in my life, certainly not Mum.'

The following evening Tessa plucked up the courage to confront her father with what she had heard and asked if he and Patricia were getting divorced. Roald exploded. He burst into a furious rage, accusing his daughter of eavesdropping and snooping into his private affairs. She later claimed that he had roared at her: 'I'm fed up with you. Get out of my house, I don't have any energy left for little bitches like you.' But then when he saw Tessa tearfully packing her bags, Roald relented and said she could stay on the condition that she would talk to Liccy and listen to her side of the story before telling her mother anything. Liccy carefully explained to Tessa that neither of them wanted to hurt Patricia, but that if she found out they would have to end their romance, which would break Roald's heart. Taking on this burden was an awful lot to ask of a teenage girl, but Tessa adored her father and agreed to keep their secret for his sake. Tessa would later go on to claim that Roald also confided 'sordid and inappropriate' details of his physical relationship with Patricia, but for the time being at least their affair could continue as it always had.

It was getting more and more difficult to hide the truth. Lucy started to wonder what was going on when Roald suddenly changed their holiday plans that summer, cancelling the usual family trip to Norway so they could join Liccy and her children in Minorca. Liccy's daughter Neisha recalled: 'It was definitely a holiday designed so Mummy and Roald could be together.' When they returned Lucy noticed that Liccy was in every one of her father's holiday photographs, and when she mentioned it to her mother Patricia confessed that she had been suspicious since catching Roald sneaking out of their bedroom one night when Liccy was staying, but had decided not to confront him: 'She opened her eyes and he froze and they just looked at each other. Both acknowledged what was happening. She turned over and went back to sleep,' Lucy said.

When Ophelia went to visit Liccy's daughters she noticed there were bottles of wine from her father's cellar in the flat, then Neisha spotted Roald's favourite Bendick's mints in the cupboard and Charlotte found aeroplane tickets for Roald in her mother's bedside drawer.

Despite all the lies and deceit, Roald and Liccy were falling deeper and deeper in love, they spoke all the time and were together as often as they could manage it but Liccy was sure Roald would never be able to bring himself to leave either the children, or his writing hut, which he insisted was a vital tool if he was to stand any chance of maintaining his professional success. Whenever Liccy was away Roald would send her impassioned love letters, although many of them have since been destroyed, in one he wrote: 'Great times, marvellous times. Easily the best times of my own particular life and how can I possibly thank you enough for that. Only I think, by loving you a tremendous amount, which is what I do.'

It all came out when Roald humiliated Patricia by inviting his lover to join them for yet another dinner at the Curzon House Club. Feeling excluded from her own marriage, Patricia felt unable to ignore her doubts any longer. The next day she asked Tessa if she though her father might be having an affair with Liccy, and Tessa revealed what she knew. She confronted her husband who seemed relieved that it was all finally out in the open, and Patricia claimed he showed 'bizarre delight in my distress'. Patricia was so furious that she immediately told Ophelia that her beloved father had 'betrayed' her, leaving the 11-year-old bewildered and distressed. Roald invited Liccy to Gipsy House the following day to help him convince Patricia that she was overreacting since Roald had no interest in filing for a divorce. Patricia felt she was being pressured into accepting his infidelity as a normal part of being married to such a passionate man. Roald pointed out that she had always known he had a very open attitude when it came to sex; Liccy felt terrible for the pain she had caused and simply added that the situation left them all deeply unhappy.

Roald had been bought up with a very permissive attitude to sex, his mother had always allowed his sisters' boyfriends to stay overnight in their house, and insisted that the subject was never taboo. When his sisters Alfhild and Else were much younger they had both slept with the same man, Dennis Pearl, who later went on to marry Else's daughter Lou when she was 18 and he was 53. Patricia had been appalled at the unconventional nature of the marriage, but Roald simply said he was pleased to have his old friend Dennis back in the family again. And guests at Gipsy House also recalled how Roald would sometimes retire to bed early, leaving notes out for his wife saying, 'If you want to fuck, wake me up.'

And now Roald appeared not to understand why Patricia should have a problem with him sleeping with another woman, but she did not share his unusual outlook on such matters. Since her stroke Patricia had lost her sexual libido and she was deeply hurt by her husband seeming to take matters into his own hands. Liccy however was wracked with guilt and told Roald she felt she had no choice but to end the affair, and wrote to Patricia apologising for her mistake: 'I feel very sad at the unhappiness which I have caused you, and hope that in the fullness of time, life will sort itself out,' she said.

Roald was heartbroken without her and missed Liccy so desperately that in 1975 he begged Patricia for her permission to see her again. He knew that Liccy would not want to sneak around behind her back again, and so Roald composed a long and heartfelt letter to Patricia asking that he be allowed to carry on living with her but still meet up with his lover occasionally. He pointed out that it would only be for a short time anyway, since he knew

Liccy would be unlikely to put up with such an unsatisfactory arrangement for very long. He wrote:

> I shall probably look occasionally for her companionship. It is not sex. You think it is. I promise you it isn't. I am very happy right now without sex of any sort. In that respect I somehow feel very tired. So what I would like to do is go on living with you and having you return this love without feeling the least bit jealous of the fact that, now and again, but not very often, I meet Liccy and have lunch with her. All of this is obviously a rotten deal for Liccy, and I sort of hope she won't put up with it for long. There is no future in it for her. I have told her long ago that there is no chance of me ever leaving you. So there is no future for her with me. For her sake though, as well as for mine, the thing should be allowed to tick over until it comes to a natural end. And the best thing you can do to encourage that ending is to be non-jealous and normal.

Patricia refused his extraordinary wish and they reached a deadlock.

Chapter Sixteen

Patricia could not bring herself to allow Roald to have an affair and he knew Liccy would not see him without her permission and so the torrid affair dwindled away to nothing for the next two years. It was agony for Roald. He missed Liccy terribly and was frustrated and angry with Patricia. His friends and even the children were concerned about the state he was in. In attempt to cheer him up in the summer of 1975 the family took their annual holiday to Norway, knowing Roald usually loved it there, but he was still miserable. It would be the last time they would all be together.

As the eldest child, Tessa was the most keenly aware of the tensions between her parents and she started to rebel even more drastically than she had done at boarding school. She threw herself into a series of unsuitable relationships with much older men, often around the same age as her father whom she felt ignored her. The most controversial fling she embroiled herself in was with the famous actor Peter Sellers, who was 50 at the time. In despair Roald moved her into the house he had bought in south London in the hope she might grow up and find a job. She had told him that she wanted to work in modelling or acting, but by the time she was 19 she was living with another actor, Julian Holloway, and within a year she had given birth to their daughter Sophie.

His first grandchild was a welcome distraction from pining for Liccy and Roald doted on Sophie from the moment she was born, but was alarmed by Tessa's unstable and bohemian lifestyle. Theo had also dropped out of school and was living at home, being schooled by a private tutor. His brain injuries made learning difficult and he seemed more content at home, often greeting Roald's guests at the door and serving them drinks.

Miraculously, Roald's two younger daughters Ophelia and Lucy managed to escape from the string of family disasters relatively unscathed, they did not remember Theo or Patricia's accidents and they recalled a different time after Tessa left home, when their father escaped from his worries by playing with them. No longer spending all his spare time with Liccy, he spent hours telling them stories again, just as he had done in the past when the others were very little. One of the children's favourite memories of his wonderful bedtime stories was the time when their father climbed up a ladder outside the house and poked a long cane through their bedroom window and told them the story of 'a big friendly giant' who lived in the orchard and blew happy dreams into their bedroom through a pipe while they slept. Although the girls did not believe in the giant, they played along because they could not bear to disappoint their fragile father: 'He seemed to me, even then, to have a vulnerable core. So I said nothing,' Ophelia recalled.

Roald often revisited this lovable character, who would of course became so well known in *The BFG* , but he first appeared in another story that Roald was working on at the time, called *Danny The Champion of the World*. Published in 1975 it was the story of the touchingly close relationship between a 9-year-old boy and his single father, a car mechanic, who was based on a combination of Roald himself, his old pal Claud, and the car dealer Gordon Hawes from his previous story *Fifty Thousand Frogskins*. Just like Roald and Claud had done, Danny's father poached pheasants with raisins laced with sleeping pills, and was prepared to break the law if it seemed unfair to him. And just as Danny's father let his son drive his customers' cars while they were being repaired at his garage; Roald had taken an equally lax approach to the law when he taught Ophelia to drive a battered old Morris Minor when she was just 10 years old, and was not particularly angry when he discovered she was sneaking off to visit friends in the car just a year later.

Danny knew his father adored him, but that he had secrets and 'powerful yearnings' that led him to disappear during the night. In the book, when Danny realised his father was far from perfect he said:

> Grown ups are complicated creatures, full of quirks and secrets. Some have quirkier quirks and deeper secrets than others, but all of them, including one's own parents, have two or three private habits hidden in their sleeves that would probably make you gasp if you knew about them.

Roald dedicated the story to 'the whole family', even though his marriage was slowly falling apart. Danny's father's nocturnal secret was that he was a poacher, while Roald's own private shortcomings were considerably harder for the children to understand. He was frustrated and started writing stories for adults littered with references to sexual frustration and dysfunction. Sex had never really appeared in his flying stories, but since being kept apart from Liccy, he started to create characters who had fallen prey to cunning, manipulative female predators. He even wrote to Charles Marsh explaining that he wanted to expose women, 'For the brutal lascivious creatures that they really are. The poor man is really nothing but a little body of skin and bones growing inconspicuously out of the base of an enormous prick which he can't even call his own.'

In a television series he wrote called *Way Out*, Roald compared men to frogs and spiders, adding that females were: 'A half-blind savage carnivore who will eat any insect she can get hold of including the male of the species.' And a collection of short stories called *Switch Bitch* featured the humorous sexual exploits of a buccaneering playboy character known as Uncle Oswald, who famously boasted: 'But tell me truly, did you ever see a sexual organ quite so grand as me?' The story was tinged with bitterness and Roald admitted he was running out of ideas for adult fiction.

In a letter sent to his former publisher Alfred Knopf just before he turned 60, Roald explained how much pleasure *Danny The Champion of the World* had given him, adding:

> I do not believe that any writer of adult books, however successful or celebrated he may be, has ever gotten half the pleasure I have got from my children's books. The readers are so incredibly responsive and enthusiastic and excited, it's a real joy to know that this is one's own doing.

Without Liccy to inspire him or to discuss new ideas with, Roald felt creatively stunted. He still longed to publish a massively successful adult novel, or at least something for older children or teenagers, but could not seem to progress beyond short stories. He lacked motivation and his next collection called *The Wonderful Story of Henry Sugar and Six More* was about a character who made lots of money but was repulsed by it.

Roald tried to forget about Liccy but it was impossible. He was still desperately in love with her and being forced apart was excruciating. He would sometimes drive ten minutes out of the village to call her from his usual phone box, but when she would not speak to him he would go home and pour his heart out to her in anguished letters instead. After one telephone call he wrote:

> I wanted to make the bell jangle all around your flat and tell your ghost that I was still here and longing for you. Are you

lying in the sun and browning those long lovely legs of yours? I am sitting in my orchard hut drinking coffee from my thermos and telling myself I must start my third short story for children. This one will be about a boy who discovered he could make objects across the room move ever so slightly by staring at them. And last night I dreamed of a marvellous chicken that grew beautiful flowers on itself instead of feathers.

I rather like that. I rather like you too. I more than rather like you. I love you.

Roald did his best to focus on his family duties and responsibilities, supervising the children, and taking over the running of the household entirely; Patricia could not be relied upon and guests were often surprised to find Roald in the kitchen organising meals as well as putting the children to bed. He kept himself busy in his orchid house where he tended to his precious collection of rare plants, and although he was lonely, exhausted, and his health was gradually fading Roald could not bring himself to leave Gipsy House. He wanted to be near Olivia's grave.

In 1977 he had a hip replacement operation but Patricia was still not really well enough to take care of him properly and he felt more alone than ever. In a moment of sheer desperation he called Liccy and insisted that he simply must see her. He sounded so frantic that Liccy was worried and drove to the house immediately. They fell into each other's arms and their affair started up again. They would meet in secret as often as they could, whenever he could claim to have a meeting in London or away on a business trip, with Liccy using the name Fiona Curzon when they checked into hotels.

Unless he was meeting her, Roald hated having to leave the house for any other reason. When he was forced to disrupt his routine to make a trip to London to surprise Patricia for an episode of the television programme *This Is Your Life* in 1978, Roald's displeasure was clear for the world to see. As a stream of smiling stars from Hollywood and the theatrical world greeted Patricia enthusiastically, and gushed about her astonishing recovery, Roald sat grumpily refusing to participate in the celebrations. Even though they were being filmed, Roald did not even try and conceal how he really felt about his wife; at one point the cameras picked up on Patricia reaching for her husband's hand, and him stuffing it back in his pocket. She was mortified and humiliated by his behaviour, but Roald refused to play along with the public charade any longer.

When asked about his dark moods Patricia explained that she knew he was a difficult man but was used to his angry outbursts and stubborn behaviour, and said: 'Success did not mellow my husband. Quite the contrary, it only enforced his conviction that although life was a two-lane street, he had the right of way.'

Roald deeply resented Patricia for depriving him of his greatest pleasure, he ached for Liccy physically and yearned for the fascinating conversations they had when they snatched time together. Years of unsuccessful surgery on his back had taken its toll as well, nothing had been able to really ease the pain, and he had physically shrunk by two inches as a result of all the surgery. Roald could no longer find the energy to conceal his profound unhappiness from the outside world. He was drinking heavily to numb the agony and when he had to go back into hospital yet again, this time for a second hip replacement and another operation on his spine, he told Ophelia that he would be glad of the peace, and a break from the mundane routine of his domestic duties.

In 1979 he was invited to participate in the radio series *Desert Island Discs* and had to choose which of his favourite records he would take with him if he were stranded on a desert island. During the interview he admitted that he secretly longed to find himself alone in the middle of nowhere: 'I hate to say it, but I would love it,' Roald confessed.

Roald lived for his occasional rendezvous with Liccy but they were unable to keep their illicit meetings secret for long, and when Ophelia called her father in a Glasgow hotel room, Liccy answered the phone without thinking. Ophelia immediately recognised Liccy's voice and although she was initially furious that their father had been lying to them again, she also felt some relief that he would have some joy back in his life. She appreciated how much he needed Liccy and was sympathetic when she discovered later why they had gone to Scotland. Liccy's daughter Charlotte had been in a serious car crash, and was lying in hospital in a coma, with a severely fractured skull. In her hour of need, Liccy had called Roald, admitting she needed him just as much as he needed her. Charlotte was all that mattered now, and the children had no choice but to accept what was going on. Ophelia visited Charlotte several times as she recovered from the accident, and witnessed the tenderness of their affair at first hand: 'It was the biggest love story ever. I felt hurt but I don't know another couple who were ever so much in love,' Ophelia said.

She and Lucy hated keeping a secret from their mother but when they saw how much more joyful their father was whenever his lover was around.

They knew their parents marriage had been dead for years, and that he needed someone to look after him since the six operations on his weakened spine had left him increasingly frail. The girls agreed that he should be with his lover if it made him happy, and Roald urged Liccy to give up the job which took her away from him so often. He loathed the film industry, which he said was a 'ruthless, horrible, druggy world', and encouraged her to retrain as a gilder so she would not have to travel so much and could work closer to him. Liccy readily agreed and after taking a craft course she set up her own company with some friends.

Before long Patricia's own suspicions reared up again, she had worked out what was going on and was brimming with bitterness and resentment, especially when she realised that the children wanted Liccy to save their father from his dark spiral of despair. Ophelia said:

> My mother had been abandoned and it felt like we were drowning. It wasn't her fault. She too had loved gardening and antiques but their marriage was sour, old and she had started to resent his talents and his love of solitude. She could do very little on her own and he was still looking after her as he was growing old. He was tired and she was angry with him. She couldn't forgive him for loving Liccy and for lying and now she felt discarded by her husband and her children. It was a terrible conundrum to be in as adolescents. We tried to make it up to Mom but she saw us all as traitors. How could we love the woman who had betrayed her?

Patricia no longer felt welcome in her own home and in 1979 agreed to give a series of lucrative lectures all over America, but her schedule was gruelling and she eventually found herself taking refuge in a monastery in Bethlehem, Connecticut, which Gary Cooper's daughter Maria had recommended to her. She enjoyed the tranquillity and the chance to reflect on how she really felt about what was going on at home. It was at the peaceful monastery that she was able to come to terms with the fact that her marriage had failed. Ophelia, Lucy and Theo flew out to join her but Roald stayed at home, finally forcing her to accept that it really was over for good. The same summer Patricia visited Martha's Vineyard for the first time and loved the island so much that in 1980 she bought a house in Edgartown and made one last attempt to salvage her marriage by asking Roald if he would consider coming to live there with her. Roald felt he owed it to Patricia to at least take a look at the new house, but he hated the place and only stayed a few days before flying straight home. The press had noticed that the Dahls appeared to be living separate lives and when Roald returned to Boston airport reporters were waiting to ask him what was going on. He stopped to explain: 'People get tired of being with each other for years – day in, day out. They need some time away from each other.'

When he got home, exhausted from the stressful journey back across the Atlantic with Theo, he wrote to Patricia, unable to maintain the charade any longer. He was 65 years old, and did not want to spend whatever years he had left stuck in a loveless marriage. The rather sad and pitiful letter he sent to her new address on Martha's Vineyard did not explicitly mention his desire to be with Liccy, but it was crystal clear he no longer wanted to be married to Patricia. He wrote:

> I long to sit quietly in Gipsy House which I adore, writing my books and stories which I adore more and playing snooker a couple of times a week which I also adore, and popping up to London twice a week to play blackjack for which I have a passion. Those things are what I like doing in my retarded physical condition. I really do feel that my travelling days are virtually over.
>
> The Vineyard is not my cup of tea. I would be totally dishonest if I said it was. Neither the heat, nor the crowds nor my inability to do my work make it congenial. The burden of my song is that everybody please excuse me from travelling far distances anymore. I'm not up to it and it's time I said so.
>
> I love everyone in the family, especially you, but just let the old boy vegetate in his surroundings.

Patricia left him in peace, only returning to Gipsy House for Christmas 1980 but the atmosphere was even more poisonous than anyone could remember. After several days of unbearable tension, Roald announced that he was seeing Liccy again. Patricia was embarrassed and angrily told Roald that she wished he were dead. She flew back to America the next day, to be forever haunted by one final chilling image of her husband – as she left through the airport departure gate she glanced around at her family, only to catch Roald roaring with laughter. 'It was the most horrendous sight of my life,' she said. 'He looked like Satan. I did not turn back again.'

Chapter Seventeen

More than a year later the split was still not finalised as Patricia was worried about money and convinced that Roald intended to leave her with nothing. Eventually Tessa and her new husband James Kelly convinced Patricia to file for divorce and get it over with, and in July 1983 the split was formally granted in a London court almost thirty years after their wedding. Neither Patricia nor Roald were present for the hearing, which did not reveal any details about Roald's infidelity or difficult behaviour. Patricia kept their apartment on Manhattan's Upper East Side but insisted that Roald's team of ruthless lawyers had left her with far less than she deserved in the divorce settlement. That Christmas, Roald invited her back to Gipsy House to celebrate with the children, and said she could take whatever she wanted, but begged her to leave Olivia's paintings for him. Liccy was free to move in and at last Roald had his dream, and insisted he was happier than he had been for years, although to the outside world he still appeared as cantankerous and difficult as ever. His chronic back pain was still troubling him and he took to firing off angry letters to the newspapers, complaining about everyday nuisances and trivial matters that frequently sent him into a rage:

> My foibles are legion, I become easily bored in the company of adults. I drink too much whisky and wine in the evenings. I eat far too much chocolate. I smoke too many cigarettes. I am bad tempered when my back is hurting. I do not always clean my finger nails. I no longer tell my children long stories at bedtime. I bet on horses and lose money that way. I dislike Mother's Day and Father's Day and all the other Days and all the cards that people buy and send out. I hate my own birthday. I am going bald.

He also grumbled about the lack of homework given in schools, X-ray machines in airports failing to detect his steel hips, television companies failing to boycott the Moscow Olympics, police brutality, the fatwa on Salman Rushdie and the war in Lebanon. He was offered an OBE in 1985 but delighted in publicly turning it down – claiming he would only accept a knighthood so that his wife could be Lady Dahl. He often railed against the establishment, although he was a great fan of Margaret Thatcher and once bought her flowers.

Roald cared less and less about whom he offended, and dinner guests were warned to brace themselves for deeply personal lines of questioning about their views on sex, religion, money or politics. He could be wildly insensitive and dominated conversations, making it increasingly clear that no subject was off limits as his notoriously short fuse appeared to be getting even shorter.

Theo explained in an interview:

> Dad had a good temper and he had a bad temper. He would tell you if he didn't like something – just flat out. He had his feelings about everybody, opinions. It was either yes or no. He liked breaking the rules, but he always liked to be right. He was a very self-opinionated man.

Ophelia added that her father often liked to be controversial just for the sake of stirring up a debate, and enjoyed picking fights with many of his children's friends: 'There was always a lack of sophistication to my father's arguments,' she said.

The more he drank, the more shocking his opinions would become, with increasingly vulgar language peppering his tirades, and it did not bother him who could hear. He behaved just as boorishly in restaurants as he did at home. Entertaining became a kind of sport for Roald but he found he increasingly had neither the time nor the inclination to run the kitchen himself, so hired a South African cook called Callie Ash who was horrified by her new boss when they met initially. When he picked her up from the station on her first day, Roald attacked her for being a privileged white settler, and when her mother handed him bottles of South African wine as a present, he poured them down the sink in disgust. But his brusque attitude thawed quickly and Callie soon became part of the family. When she needed to show the British authorities she had funds of £150,000 available to apply for citizenship, Roald immediately wrote her a cheque for the full amount and left it in her bank account for years.

Roald went out of his way to ensure he was the centre of attention both privately and professionally, and so when he felt that his publisher Rayner Unwin was not lavishing him with as much praise as he felt he deserved for *Danny The Champion of the World*, he announced that he would be moving to rival publishing house Jonathan Cape. Unwin was very understanding since Jonathan Cape had a specialist children's department and offered him huge royalties on the sales of hardback books. The main focus of Roald's literary affairs had moved from New York to London although he still had moments when he felt like an outsider on the UK publishing scene. Roald was convinced that he was not considered a mainstream author because his most successful books were written for children, and often sensed he was being excluded by what he saw as the intellectual and artistic elite. It left him feeling vulnerable and insecure, despite being a commercial money-maker.

But he was right in thinking that many literary critics looked down their noses at *Charlie and the Chocolate Factory*, which was branded vulgar, brash and tasteless, and some feared there was a danger that the greedy, spoilt and grotesque characters could encourage children to behave badly. Publishers who had turned the book down boasted about what a wise decision they had made in hindsight, while some bookshops and librarians actually refused to stock it on their shelves. Roald thought the backlash was ridiculous, but it was about to get a lot worse.

When plans for the film adaptation were announced the National Association for the Advancement of Colored People (NAACP) objected to the project on the grounds that the book was racist, suggesting that the Oompa Loompas who ran Willy Wonka's factory were portrayed as African pygmies. Roald was shocked as he had never intended to cause any offence. In the book he had written that the workers came 'from the deepest and darkest part of the jungle where no white man had ever been before'. But Roald had not appreciated quite how ferociously the social tide was turning in the aftermath of the book's publication, particularly in America where the Black Panther movement was on the rise and Martin Luther King had just been shot. Many felt that the Oompa Loompas reinforced a negative stereotype of slavery that the black community was trying hard to overcome. Since the word chocolate had implied racist undertones too, the film's producers found themselves under increasing pressure to remove the characters altogether and change the title of the movie to avoid the backlash. Roald offered to make the Oompa Loompas white but the NAACP argued the change did not go far enough, and if the film was successful it would further promote sales of the original book.

Roald wrote to his old friend Alfred Knopf saying: 'The book is banned by the NAACP. They thought I was writing a subtle anti-negro manual. But such a thing had never crossed my mind.'

Roald omitted to mention that he had initially considered making Charlie black, but eventually both sides agreed that the Oompa Loompas would become little people with green hair and orange skin, while the film's title would be altered slightly to *Willy Wonka and the Chocolate Factory*. It was the first of many things Roald would eventually dislike about the film. He thought the songs were trashy and the script had been watered down so much it lost 'a good deal of the bite'. He complained that the script focused far too much on Willy Wonka and not enough on the character of Charlie Bucket. Roald was also disappointed in the performance of the lead actor Gene Wilder, whom he found pretentious – he had lobbied hard for a British comedian, either Spike Milligan or Peter Sellers, to be cast as Wonka.

He earnt a hefty $300,000 writer's fee, but the episode confirmed the worst of Roald's firmly held fears about working in the movie industry and he dreaded having to promote it enthusiastically in press interviews when it was released. He would later disown the film, pulling his name from the project entirely. But the storm of controversy gained Roald further notoriety since anything that irritated teachers or librarians seemed to delight children, and book sales continued to soar. Fearing further problems, Roald's editors at Knopf went back through all of Roald's past work, scouring and scrutinising it for any words or phrases that they feared could potentially cause offence. When Fabio Coen questioned his use of the word 'spade' in *Fantastic Mr Fox*, Roald agreed to make changes: 'I will try and think of another word for spade. Shovel will not do because that is used in the story for mechanical shovels. Black with rage will certainly change.' He also agreed to remove a section in an early draft of the sequel *Charlie and the Great Glass Elevator* in which the President of China spoke with a silly accent on a yellow telephone, but rejected offers to adapt it into a film because he had been so disappointed with the way *Charlie and the Chocolate Factory* had ended up on screen.

From then on Roald would receive a steady stream of letters from people who found racist implications in his writing, and he largely ignored them. But he could not hold his tongue when a Canadian critic called Eleanor Cameron, published a ferocious attack on his book, calling it cheap, tasteless, ugly, sadistic and implied that reading it might actually harm children.

Roald was forced to respond this time, and he said he was horrified by her 'insensitive and monstrous implication', which, he added, was 'out of touch with reality' and that he had told his own children thousands of bedtime stories over the years without doing them any harm. Another critic, Ursula K. Le Guin wrote a piece saying her 'usually amiable daughter became quite nasty' after reading *Charlie and the Chocolate Factory*, and Roald said it was so hurtful he almost considered giving up writing altogether.

Luckily the criticism that came his way was vastly outweighed by the sacks of fan mail he received each week, and Roald did his best to send out dozens of postcards in response to the children who contacted him with all kinds of questions and compliments. Sometimes he sent longer letters to children, encouraging them if they showed an early interest in writing themselves, or if they sent him a particularly honest or funny review. Thanking one child for posting feedback on a story he wrote: 'Up to now, a whole lot of grown-ups have written reviews, but none of them have really known what they were talking about because a grown-up talking about a children's book is like a man talking about a woman's hat.'

Meanwhile Roald was raking in a small fortune from a batch of twisted tales which was adapted by Anglia television into a long running drama series called *Roald Dahl's Tales of the Unexpected*, and each episode was introduced on camera by Roald himself. There was a huge demand for more and more episodes, as the series aired from 1979 until 1988. In need of a break from TV he snapped up a request from *Playboy* to write another story about his character Uncle Oswald for the magazine's twenty-fifth anniversary. He quickly produced what he later described as 'the longest and dirtiest' story he had ever written. The protagonist was a pathetic creature, entirely dominated by the needs of his penis, and Roald quite obviously relished exposing the ridiculous nature of male sexual behaviour through Oswald's ridiculous attempts to seduce women – which included secretly adding a love potion to truffles made by Roald's favourite chocolate shop, Prestat in London.

When asked if he saw anything of himself in Uncle Oswald, Roald later replied: 'I would like to have been like him and I think that all men would like to be like him.'

Another bonus for Roald was that *My Uncle Oswald* formed the first of four books he owed his publishers as part of a convoluted new deal he had signed in order to get round the American IRS tax requirements. His accountants had come up with a semi-legitimate way of avoiding tax in both the UK and the US on the hefty royalty payments he was earning from foreign book sales. Under the terms of the new payment deal Roald would be paid in four large instalments, as advances for new books, rather than receiving royalties on sales at random as he had before. Roald was confused by all the legal jargon, hated having to plough through complicated contracts and generally avoided getting embroiled in the business side of things. But he understood that he was now under pressure to deliver new material fast if he wanted his money.

It was good news for the publisher because it meant their star author was tied to them. The second and third books would be *The Twits* and *George's Marvellous Medicine*, both guaranteed hits as long as they could find an illustrator that Roald felt was worthy of a large slice of his royalties. He had not yet met the legendary Quentin Blake whose distinctive sharp drawings would soon become synonymous with Roald's words.

While the two new stories he submitted went down exceptionally well, Roald's hardworking team of American editors at Random House were growing tired of his haughty attitude, the way he furiously objected to changes they dared to suggest, and his angry tirades if there was any delay on his payments. Roald was getting the distinct impression that he was no longer being treated as their number one priority, and the final straw came when Bob Gottleib appeared too busy to respond to his request for new pencils. Roald had been using Dixon Ticonderoga pencils since he began writing thirty-seven years earlier, but Gottleib was not in the habit of buying stationery for his authors and Roald's increasingly frantic demands were ignored for three months. When an assistant eventually sent him a close alternative to the specific pencils he wanted, Roald was incandescent with rage at being treated in such a shoddy way. The pencils were crucially important to him and not that hard to come by in New York. He felt the assistant had not tried hard enough to help, which he took to mean that he therefore was not sufficiently valued at Random House. The relationship between Roald and everyone who dealt with him were becoming strained to breaking point. As tensions ran high Gottleib warned Roald that his demands were 'exaggerated, dotty, unrealistic and unmeetable'.

In August 1980, Roald sent the last of the four books; a collection of hilariously repulsive poems called *Dirty Beasts*, and hoped that would release him from his contract. He wrote angrily to Gottleib:

> I would like to hear from you or from someone that the nefarious four book contract between Knopf and the foreign company has now been completed. That would be a small act of grace and thoughtfulness. I have felt that fucking contract clutching at my throat like a bloodsucking vampire ever since it was written.

Roald received his payment as agreed but from then on he was irritated by everything from the size of his name on the jacket of *The Twits* to the layout of the illustrations. He felt insulted that Gottleib had washed his hands of him, having passed on his work to the head of the juvenile department, Frances Foster. Needless to say Foster was thrilled to inherit Roald, but the feeling was not mutual and the harder she tried to pacify him the more irate he became.

Replying to one of his many complaints about the design of *The Twits* she told him:

> I wish we could keep you happy! I can't tell you how much it distresses me to have you disappointed. For me, it goes without saying that you are THE author on the list we most want to please – and it seems we don't do a very good job of it.

Despite having been with Random House and Knopf in its various guises since 1943, Roald threatened to leave as soon as *Dirty Beasts* was published. He probably expected them to put up a fight, but Gottleib had grown tired of Roald's overbearing manner and the way he directed abuse at many of his staff who did not deserve his ire. He wrote:

> You have behaved to us in a way I can honestly say is unmatched in my experience for overbearingness and utter lack of civility. For a while I put your behaviour down to the physical pain you were in and so managed to excuse it. Now I've come to believe that you're just enjoying a prolonged tantrum and are bullying us.
>
> Your threat to leave Knopf after this current contract is fulfilled leaves us far from intimidated. I will be sorry to see you depart, for business reasons, but these are not strong enough to make us put up with your manner to us any longer. You've managed to make the entire experience of publishing you unappealing for all of us – counter-productive I would have thought.
>
> To be perfectly clear, let me reverse your threat: unless you start acting civilly towards us, there is no possibility of our agreeing to publish you.

Gottleib revealed afterwards that when he sent the letter everyone at Random House stood up and cheered. He was convinced by then that the problem stemmed from anti-Semitism on Roald's part: 'At one point it became clear that he thought we were just a bunch of blood-sucking Jews,' he said. 'We were Jews, but very generous. Everyone had gone out of his way to keep Roald happy and give him what he wanted. He was clearly out of control.'

Two days later Roald wrote to Alfred Knopf, who was by then 89 years old and had virtually nothing to do with the day-to-day running of the company, to express his dismay at the way he had been treated:

> I am, as I hope you know, a very easy man to get on with, and in my thirty-seven years of writing have never before had a row with a single publisher. I live quietly in the country and get on with my business. It is only when someone really does behave very badly to me that I become aroused. I certainly would not try to bully a publisher or throw my weight around.

Although there is no written record of Roald specifically mentioning the fact that Gottleib and Bernstein were Jewish in any of the letters he sent – and he would very rarely make transatlantic phone calls – two years later he aired a similar view and was accused of anti-Semitism again. In 1982 Roald reviewed a book called *God Cried* about the Israeli army invading Beirut. Australian war reporter Tony Clifton had taken a series of harrowing photographs showing the large numbers of innocent victims of the warfare. Tessa thought the book might interest her father as he had donated generously to Palestinian educational charities in the past; and the proceeds of the charity premiere of Patricia's film *Hud* were sent to Palestinian refugees in Ramallah. Tessa was right, and Roald wrote a lengthy critique entitled *Not A Chivalrous Affair*. But it was a piece that would tarnish his reputation forever:

> In June 1941, I happened to be in, of all places, Palestine, flying with the RAF against the Vichy French and the Nazis. Hitler happened to be in Germany and the gas-chambers were being built and the mass slaughter of Jews was beginning. Our hearts bled for the Jewish men, women and children, and we hated the Germans.
>
> Exactly forty-one years later, in June 1982, the Israeli forces were screaming northwards out of what used to be Palestine into Lebanon, and the mass slaughter of the inhabitants began.

Our hearts bled for the Lebanese and Palestinian men, women and children, and we all started hating the Israelis.

It was the kind of inflammatory opinion Roald was used to airing, but he usually saved his ranting for private debates, and when the piece was published it caused offence in ways he had certainly not imagined. There was widespread condemnation of the way he compared Israel to Nazi Germany. Liccy was also horrified when she saw it, and urged him to make amends but he refused and the couple left for a pre-planned holiday, a surprising decision which appeared to show a staggering lack of remorse. When they returned Roald was bombarded with furious letters and phone calls, and discovered he had been branded an anti-Semite around the globe.

Roald accepted that he should try and clear the mess up, but the bungling attempts he made to set the record straight simply made matters worse. First he wrote a letter to *The Times*, explaining that to his mind, calling him anti-Jewish was as foolish as calling him anti-Arab because he had also been critical of Colonel Gaddafi. 'I am not anti-Semitic. I am anti-Israel,' he wrote. He then gave a telephone interview to *The New Statesman* in which he talked about 'a trait in the Jewish character that does provoke a certain animosity, maybe it's a kind of lack of generosity towards non-Jews. Even a stinker like Hitler didn't pick on them for no reason.'

Even when Roald desperately needed to appear consolatory, sensitive and contrite, he was as blunt and tactless as ever. There had been previous occasions when Roald had gleefully revealed his true colours to friends, leaving his family squirming with embarrassment. He enjoyed shocking people and did not care if he annoyed or upset them; in particular he relished crucifying his daughters' boyfriends at the dinner table. Roald certainly did not believe in political correctness, he could be cruel and it would have never crossed his mind to change or even temper his view in case it was unpopular or anti-intellectual. For years his outrageous slurs and offensive generalisations had become par for the course at home, but this was the first time the public had been made aware of it, and other examples started to emerge.

Some time earlier he had written to his friend Dirk Bogarde describing an American film producer as 'The wrong sort of Jew,' adding an unflattering description worthy of a villain in one of his books: 'His face is matted with dirty, black hair. He is disgustingly overweight and flaccid though only forty-something, garrulous, egocentric, arrogant, complacent, ruthless, dishonourable, lascivious, slippery.'

But he did not save his fury just for the Jews – he had also plenty to irritate him about the French, Dutch, Germans, Swedes, Irish, Iraqis and Americans. Those closest to him had come to ignore most of it, understanding that for Roald, feisty debates were little more than sport. His Jewish friend Sir Isaiah Berlin said: 'I thought he might say anything. Could have been pro-Arab or pro-Jew. There was no consistent line. He was a man who followed whims, which meant he would blow up in one direction, so to speak.

Amelia Foster, who later became director of the Roald Dahl Museum in Great Missenden, agreed:

> This is again an example of how Dahl refused to take anything seriously, even himself. He was very angry at the Israelis. He had a childish reaction to what was going on in Israel. Dahl wanted to provoke, as he always provoked at dinner. His publisher was a Jew, his agent was a Jew … and he thought nothing but good things of them. He asked me to be his managing director, and I'm Jewish.

And Ophelia added:

> I learned early on that he wasn't interested in the matter of the argument. He simply wanted to cause a stir. I wasn't keen on his rather more controversial public side. Some of it was about very strongly held opinions and some that I respect a lot because he really didn't do things in order to be popular, and he didn't say things so that he could gain public approval. In fact, if he felt strongly about something, he would say it often really without thinking about the consequences very much or who he might be hurting.

Chapter Eighteen

Roald always had a strong sense that he was an outsider, a feeling that had followed him ever since his public schooldays when he was surrounded by minor aristocracy and the ruling classes. He certainly did not fit in among City commuters and often felt uneasy among the RAF officers and high ranking British diplomats he worked with later. Without a birthright or family name to answer to he never felt any sense of responsibility and had become quite fearless about expressing his opinions. As a child, his mother and sister had indulged and adored him, his schoolmasters turned a blind eye to his acts of rebellion and women had always forgiven his infidelity and thoughtless behaviour. He had a way of charming his way out of trouble and so when public opinion turned against him he felt that everyone else was simply failing to understand his point of view.

Roald could rarely be persuaded to apologise, change his mind or back down, but on this occasion he did eventually admit that the piece had been written 'so fast and so emotionally'. What mattered to him was making his point, and he resented being censored by the outside world. He actually felt that he should be commended for how often he held himself back from revealing some of his darkest thoughts. He said in an interview: 'Every writer should be his own censor – up to a point. All of us should exercise a degree of censorship. In my children's books there's a wild degree of censorship. I eschew all sexual matters. And violence as well.'

He often came out with strong opinions that he did not really believe, just to be controversial, and did not care if anyone agreed with him or not, he just enjoyed the debate. He had very little respect for authority, and would openly disagree with his bosses, editors and teachers at his children's schools.

There are very few examples of times when Roald backed down from one of his contentious standpoints, although he did come to regret being rude to the headmistress of Ophelia and Lucy's junior school, Goldstone, and in a rare moment of self-awareness he wrote to her: 'My trouble is I get so carried away by it all, I forget completely the impact these things may have upon the reader.'

 Despite the reputation he was gathering among literary circles and the wider public for being unpleasant and racist, Roald always had a strong sense of social justice. When he spotted policemen beating up a black man who was resisting arrest in London's Hyde Park in 1988, he filed a formal complaint against the officers for brutality. He thought it was desperately unfair and agreed to be a witness when the case went to court, but the case was dropped after the police pointed out that he was a fiction writer who was used to making up or exaggerating stories. Other witnesses contradicted his version of events but Roald felt he had been misunderstood, and felt that, like his character the Big Friendly Giant, his words did not come out as he had intended. As the years went by, Roald found it increasingly difficult to communicate satisfactorily with adults. Approaching 70, he found it easier to understand how children's minds worked: 'It is no easy matter for the adult to recall totally and with absolute clarity some forty or fifty years later just what it was like to be a little boy, or a little girl. I can do it. I am certain I can,' he said.

He knew his work was sneered at by highbrow literary critics but Roald felt more certain than ever that he knew what children wanted from him. Piles of adoring letters from his legions of young fans arrived every day, confirming that millions of children around the world were completely devoted to him. He would refer to himself as 'a geriatric child' and talked about himself as their representative and spokesman; he seemed to be entering his own second childhood as he happily lived out his final years with his beloved Liccy by his side. 'A kind of serenity settles upon you like a warm mist. The struggle is over,' he explained. 'Every movement becomes slower. You have all the time in the world. There is no rush. The never-ending fight to achieve something excellent has ended.'

Moving his lover into Gipsy House had not been a seamless transition. His children were expected to make way not just for Liccy, but also her three daughters, although the couple assured them all they would not be having any more children of their own. Liccy, with her keen sense of creativity and design, vowed to make the house not just more stable for the newly blended family, but also prettier and more private.

First she set about completely redesigning the garden, which Patricia had nurtured so lovingly. She replaced the barely used swimming pool and greenhouse with a separate living annex and snooker room. The drawing room on the ground floor of the main house became their master bedroom since Roald was having difficulty climbing the stairs. He complained loudly and bitterly about the noise and dust while the renovations were going on but ultimately he could see that Liccy was trying to create a more tranquil haven for them all. She was only 46 when she moved in, but was delighted to finally have the chance to look after the man she had loved for so long, and to make his final years more comfortable.

The wait was finally over and Roald married Liccy in a low-key ceremony at Brixton Town Hall in 1983 and his children were relieved to see how stimulated and fulfilled their father had become. After years of restless nights, unable to sleep for more than three or four hours at a time, he was relaxed and rejuvenated; with all the emotional, physical and financial distractions finally behind him, Roald found himself able to write more than he had managed in years. Describing the feeling of writing, Roald said:

> You become a different person, you are no longer an ordinary fellow who walks around and looks after his children and eats meals and does silly things, you go into a completely different world. Everything else in your life disappears and you look at your bit of paper and get completely lost in what you're doing. Time disappears completely.

Without any pressure on him from publishers, Roald returned to an idea he had scribbled down years earlier about a man who captured children's hopes and dreams and kept them in bottles, based on the bedtime stories he had told his daughters years ago. For an entire year he worked on nothing but *The BFG*, and dedicated it to Olivia on the twentieth anniversary of her death. In the first draft the main character was a boy called Jody, but was later changed to Sophie, after his granddaughter. It was the longest children's book he had ever written – and his favourite, and he became totally immersed in creating 'gobble funk' – the loveable giant's mangled language of words that were 'squiff squiddled around'. Sophie enlists the queen to help her defeat the child-eating giants with names including Bonecruncher, Fleshlumpeater and Bloodbottler.

Eventually he sent the first draft to his new American publisher, Stephen Roxburgh at Farrar, Straus and Giroux in New York, and asked if he had any improvements. An academic who specialised in Victorian children's literature, Roxburgh was nervous about the first time he had to deal with Roald, whose difficult reputation preceded him. However, he sent back eleven pages of notes, including detailed observations and ways to refine the giant's language. He warned that the grammatically incorrect words were bound to offend legions of parents, teachers and librarians, which would only serve to make the book even more popular with children. Roxburgh need not have worried about upsetting Roald who was thrilled at finally finding a thoughtful, enthusiastic editor who seemed to truly understand him.

He felt this was what he had been waiting for, and sent a glowing reply to Roxburgh:

> I am absolutely swishboggled and sloshbungled by the trouble you have taken and by the skill of your editorial work on *The BFG*. In nearly forty years of dealing with publishers, I have never seen a job like it. Ninety eight per cent of your comments were thoroughly sound and a couple of them were vital. 'The whole thing must have driven you round the twist. It nearly drove me the same way going through them. But it was all marvellously worthwhile. You are right that frobscottle (a delicious fizzy liquid, whose bubbles travel downwards) and whizzpoppers (extravagant noisy farts brought on by drinking frobscottle) should not be an isolated incident never to be mentioned again. So I've gone even further and had the BFG doing a whizzpopper for the Queen. Slightly vulgar perhaps, but you and I know that the children will love it. And this is a book for children. To hell with the spinster librarians of your country. By now I am impervious to their comments. The louder they shout, the better the book does.

Roxburgh was brimming with confidence that they had a hit on their hands; there could not be a shred of doubt that children would adore *The BFG* for years to come, and of course he was right. He wrote back again to Roald confidently predicting the successful outcome of their new partnership: '*The BFG* will be thoroughly successful,' he said 'I stand flabberstacked by your kind words. Praise from you is praise indeed. The new scene in which the BFG whizzpops for the Queen is simply one of the funniest things I have ever read.'

When the book hit the shelves Roald's inventive use of language was a sensation. Children too as they delighted in being able to understand the meaning of words they had never heard before because the sounds were familiar, and inundated Roald with letters written in the same style. Lexicographer Dr Susan Rennie explained:

> He didn't always explain what his words meant, but children can work them out because they often sound like a word they

know, and he loved using onomatopoeia. For example, you know that something *lickswishy* and *delumptious* is good to eat, whereas something *uckyslush* or *rotsome* is definitely not! He also used sounds that children love to say, like *squishous* and *squizzle* or *fizzlecrump* and *fizzwiggler*.

When Roxburgh mentioned that he would soon be visiting London, Roald immediately invited him to Gipsy House for lunch. As he took the train out to Buckinghamshire, Roxburgh was nervous about saying or doing something to embarrass himself, but he need not have worried because from the moment they met it was clear how much the two men had in common. They sparked off each other. As well as sharing same literary tastes, they were both keen wine buffs and equally enthusiastic about woodwork and cabinet making. The meeting was such a success that as soon as Roxburgh left Roald shut himself away in his writing hut, and the very next day drove down to London to show him the first draft of his new book *The Witches* in person.

As well as forging a close working relationship with Roxburgh, Roald was also bonding with his new illustrator. He had first worked with Quentin Blake back in 1978 when Roald had been delighted with his spiky, witty drawings for *The Enormous Crocodile*. The hideous caricatures Blake came up with for *The Twits* and *George's Marvellous Medicine* had proved equally popular but he only met Roald in person for the first time when they started working together on *The BFG*. Roald's British editor, Tom Maschler at Jonathan Cape, introduced them at his office in London, but their initial meeting did not get off to a good start. Blake was very nervous, and when Maschler said they wanted twelve illustrations for the twenty-four chapters, Roald demanded at least twice as many more, saying: 'I hope I am not right in thinking that because Quentin is sharing in the royalties of this book he has done a rather quicky job and got away with as few illustrations as possible.'

But when Roald realised that Blake was only being paid £300 in total, he was mortified that he had suggested he was only in it for the money, and insisted that Maschler increase his fee substantially in order to ensure the book was fully illustrated. They renegotiated Blake's deal and started the drawings again from scratch, with Roald explaining in great detail precisely how he imagined the giant to look, right down to his huge ears. He even sent the artist one of his own enormous Norwegian sandals to help him get the 24ft tall ogre exactly as he wanted, and described to him a great family friend called Wally Saunders who often played snooker with Roald, and even dug his grave when he died. Wally's daughter Anthea recalled: 'They always told him he looked like a giant. But then he came home and said he'd been drawn and that was it. I can see my dad in the pictures of the BFG – everyone could see it, he had such big ears and big hands.' Blake responded with affectionate enthusiasm to Roald's constant stream of suggestions. Theirs remains one of the most successful collaborations in the history of children's publishing.

Preparing *The BFG* for publication was a full-time job and Roald was exhausted, but he forged ahead with *The Witches* in tandem, and by 1984 he had yet another project on the go, *The Giraffe and the Pelly and Me* – a short story about a little boy who sets up a window cleaning operation with the help of a giraffe, a pelican and a monkey. Although it was only thirty-two pages long, in the end it took seven months to complete as Roald became obsessive about it and insisted on hundreds of rewrites. He described the whimsical story as 'the hardest thing in the world', although he loved the colourful illustrations Blake sent to accompany it.

Although he struggled to find a comfortable position in his writing chair due to the pain in his spine and having endured three agonising bowel operations, Roald soldiered on with work mostly to impress Liccy. He was only too aware of the age difference between them, and was determined to prove that he still had the ambition, energy and drive she had found so exciting when they had first met. She loved watching him work, even though he had to take breaks to rest more often than before, and was unable to tackle almost any domestic tasks in the house or the garden, although he still managed to gamble occasionally and continued to indulge his fondness for excellent wine. He was starting to find entertaining a struggle and nights out became less frequent. He cared even less than before about offending people, and refused to behave even when his publishers threw a star-studded party for him in a private dining room at the Garrick Club in Covent Garden in 1988, inviting some of his glamorous friends including Francis Bacon, the actress Joanna Lumley and broadcaster Frank Delaney. The evening was apparently going according to plan until Roald suddenly interrupted the conversation to bark that the meal was finished and he was going home: 'We all had to suddenly swallow our chocolate mousse and leave our undrunk wine and fight for our coats,' recalled Joanna Lumley. 'It was a ghastly end to a fabulous evening.'

Roald's gloom might have been down to an enormous tax bill which had just thudded onto his doormat. He had been moving money out of the country for years, depositing large amounts into Swiss bank accounts, but the Inland Revenue eventually caught up with him and after a lengthy wrangle he was slapped with a bill for £717,000. As a result, Roald was even less interested in parties than usual.

The Witches, which he dedicated to his second wife, was doing well even though he had been accused of misogyny after portraying his female characters in a deeply unflattering way once again. Most of the women he described tended to be grotesque, vicious hags who treated children cruelly. In *Matilda*, the tyrannical Mrs Trunchbull warned: 'A bad girl is a far more dangerous creature than a bad boy. What's more, they're much harder to squash. Squashing a bad girl is like trying to squash a bluebottle. You bang down on it and the darn thing isn't there.' When Roxburgh suggested it might be prudent to tone down the descriptions a little, Roald replied:

> I am not as frightened of offending women as you are. This sort of problem arises in all my children's stories and I ignore it. I must keep reminding you that this is a book for children and I don't give a bugger what grown ups think about it.

Roald decided to focus on the praise he was receiving over the moving and sensitive way he had handled the subject of death in *The Witches*. When the little boy turned into a mouse his lifespan was shortened so much that he realised he and his 86-year-old grandmother would probably die together, and they snuggled up in a tender final embrace. But Roald was furious when that pivotal scene was cut from the film adaptation. In the Warner Bros version the mouse turned back into a boy, which he felt entirely ruined the point of the story.

Early drafts of *The Witches* had also included biographical details from Roald's own childhood, including a passage about the boy travelling to Norway for magical holidays with his grandmother who told him wonderful stories. Although these chapters were cut, Roxburgh loved them and suggested that Roald recycle them in another book about his own upbringing. Although Roald had always maintained that autobiographies were 'the height of egotism', he accepted the challenge and soon a parcel arrived on Roxburgh's desk in New York containing every letter Roald had written to his mother, tied up in bundles with blue ribbons. Within a year *Boy* was ready for publication, a fascinating account of Roald's childhood containing photographs, extracts from his letters and illustrations. Children and adults devoured it and clamoured for him to write about his adult life too. Two years later *Boy* was followed up with a sequel called *Going Solo* which was equally successful, and Quentin Blake commented: 'They were hybrids of true autobiography, recollections and his own imagination. He would always take a story in a direction that made it more accurate.'

Roxburgh enjoyed editing both the books so much that Roald suggested he should write his official biography after his death. He became so important to Roald and so close to the whole family that Ophelia, who was then 21, invited Roxburgh and his girlfriend to move in to Gipsy House to research the book: 'You could stay here for the rest of your lives,' she joked. 'You could be Chief Logsman, snooker coach and write the book. Perhaps we could draw his life story out over, say, twelve volumes.'

Ophelia was in need of company since life at Gipsy House had become very quiet; Liccy made sure there were far fewer visitors than there had been when Patricia was there because Roald needed the peace. Theo was still living at home but Ophelia herself had decided to work in Third World medicine and was preparing to leave for Haiti; Tessa was living nearby with her financier husband James Kelly, Sophie – who would later go on to become an international supermodel – and their two other children Clover and Luke. Lucy had moved to Florida with her husband Michael, a man Roald disliked so intensely that in the bridal car on the morning of their marriage he had offered his daughter the entire cost of the wedding, tens of thousands of pounds, if she jilted him. Like Tessa, Lucy had gone through a rebellious phase and experimented with drugs, stealing her father's gambling money, wine from his cellar and even pawning the gold cigarette case his mother had given him before the war. She has since spoken about the cold and somewhat detached way Roald dealt with all his children, particularly during their adolescence, and how he would go to great lengths to avoid showing them affection. He would secretly go and watch them compete in sporting events but leave before the end and pretend he was never there, not realising how easy he had been to spot in the crowd. Lucy hated being sent away to boarding school so much that she once sabotaged her father's car so he could not drive her back, feigned severe headaches and eventually set fire to a building to ensure she was expelled. Roald could not cope with his wild daughter when she returned home, and sent her to live with Tessa in London for a while.

Lucy said: 'He did not know what to do with me, he had no idea. I don't think he was very interested in adolescents. He didn't like them. I don't think he could identify with them at all.' But she added that Roald was toughest on Theo: 'I watched everything,' she said. 'Dad was always pushing him too far and I think Theo felt that he was always disappointing him.' Theo drifted between numerous unsuitable jobs, only really enjoying some part-time work in a local supermarket, before moving to Florida and starting a family.

Roald did not want to discuss their problems and tended to avoid all difficult subjects with his children, although he said that attending meetings of Narcotics Anonymous should be a compulsory part of education, and in an article entitled *Things I Wish I'd Known When I Was Eighteen* he complained about promiscuity among his children's generation:

> Today a girl will 'move in' with a boy or vice versa with no more fuss than if one was moving in an old sofa. They go on holidays together without a blink and often never see each other again afterwards. I am so happy therefore, that I was not swept into this particular dustbin when I was eighteen.

But while his children were lurching from one crisis to another as they emerged from his long shadow, Roald was entirely consumed by struggling to finish his last long children's book: *Matilda*.

Chapter Nineteen

Anyone reading an early draft of *Matilda* could be forgiven for thinking that the eccentric Roald Dahl had finally lost the plot. It was the shocking and savage story of a little girl, Matilda Wormwood, who was wicked from the day she was born and spent her time gambling and cheating at the racetracks. The child had the ability to move objects with her mind but used her telekinetic powers to manipulate the result of a horserace to help her favourite teacher win money – and died doing it.

Even Roald's greatest fan, his American editor Stephen Roxburgh, brandished it 'hopeless' and could not bring himself to respond to the manuscript. Roald knew it was a mess and admitted: 'I had awful trouble with it. I got it wrong.' Roxburgh was so worried that he decided to fly over from New York to discuss the changes and revisions with Roald in person, but they disagreed constantly. Roald was so exhausted by the editing process that he announced it would be easier to simply tear the whole thing up and start again from scratch – something he had never done before. Roxburgh feared there would still be so many revisions needed that he should be paid extra, and took the highly unusual step of suggesting he had spent so long working on *Matilda* that he should be paid a percentage of the royalties. Roald was always grateful for Roxburgh's input but had never heard of an editor personally demanding royalties and was so angry that he took the final version of *Matilda* to Penguin Books instead.

Attempting to explain his sudden departure to Roxburgh, Roald wrote:

> I would be dishonest if I did not tell you that I feel pretty uncomfortable about this whole business. My duty is to my own family in the long term, and I must not allow sentiment to prevent me from getting the best terms I can for my works. Both Liccy and Ophelia agree reluctantly and with great sadness that I am right to go elsewhere now.

Roxburgh urged him not to be hasty, and not to try and negotiate a fresh contract himself, but the damage was done. He would no longer be writing Roald's biography, and after he died Roxburgh said he regretted the fall out:

> He'd involved me in his life and there was great personal affection and admiration. He was a father figure for me – there's no question about that. He dealt with superlatives, the best, the brightest, the most famous, the richest. If your star fell out of the constellation you quickly became the lowest, meanest, stupidest, vilest of things. He saw things in black and white.

Meanwhile his new editor at Penguin, Peter Mayer, swept *Matilda* off the market with glee and nailed Roald to a new deal with the children's arm of the company Puffin Books. Liz Attenborough, the head of Puffin, offered Roald a generous share of the royalties, and they struck up an instant rapport. Roald liked how she asked her own children to comment on his ideas, rather than imagining what young readers might want. And he appreciated the fact that she always picked up the phone herself when he called, without making him go through her secretary first. He had worked with dozens of editors and numerous publishing houses, but claimed that Liz was the first to show him sales charts, which thrilled him as making money was far more important to Roald than anyone had appreciated before.

Roald was justifiably proud of the final version of *Matilda*, which featured almost all his trademark touches. There were unkind adult villains who mistreated children who did not deserve it, but triumphed in the end. The horrible headmistress Miss Trunchbull, who swung girls around by their pigtails and hurled them out of the window and also punished a greedy child for his gluttony – in this case Bruce Bogtrotter was given his comeuppance for stealing by being forced to eat a gigantic chocolate cake in front of the whole school. The running theme throughout was a love of stories and books. Matilda took refuge in her local library when her mother disappeared to play bingo, telling her 'Looks is more important than books.' Matilda proves her ghastly mother wrong after meeting the librarian Mrs Phelps who encouraged her love of reading by recommending a series of classic novels. When Matilda admitted she did not understand some of the grown-up books she was reading, Mrs Phelps told her: 'Don't worry about the bits you can't understand. Sit back and allow the words to wash around you, like music.'

CHAPTER NINETEEN

The book was an instant classic, sales were through the roof and Roald had more money than he would ever need. After all the medical traumas that had plagued his family, he had saved enough to ensure they would always be able to afford the very best healthcare, and decided it was time to share his good fortune. He donated hefty sums to charities which were close to his heart, particularly those helping stroke victims and sick children – the main beneficiary was Great Ormond Street Children's Hospital in London. He was frequently contacted on behalf of sick or injured children from all around the world and wanted to help as many of them as could. One woman who asked for a signed book to help raise funds for wheelchairs for her two disabled daughters was flabbergasted when he paid for both chairs instead. He auctioned the rights of a short story called *The Vicar of Nibbleswicke* to raise funds for the Dyslexia Institute, and donated the original manuscript of *You Only Live Twice* to the writers charity PEN. He supported his nieces and nephews financially, often treating them to lavish gifts such as foreign holidays, and he even increased Patricia's divorce settlement.

Roald would go out of his way to encourage young readers too, and was most eager to help children who had limited access to books in some of the poorest parts of the world. He said:

> Sometimes it gives me a funny feeling that my writing arm
> is about six thousand miles long and that the hand that holds
> the pencil is reaching all the way across the world to faraway
> houses and classrooms where children live and go to school.
> That is a thrill all right.

He supported dozens of literary campaigns and insisted his purpose was 'To teach children to be comfortable with a book and to read a book.'

Ophelia explained: 'He liked handing money around and being generous with it. But he was consistently surprised by the sort of treats and delights that it could buy and the very serious things that money could do.'

He did not give many readings but when he did they were magical. Children adored him, and he could still hold them enthralled with his storytelling, making them gasp and roar with laughter. He once said: 'The nicest small children, without the slightest doubt, are those who have been fed upon fantasy. The nastiest are the ones who know all the facts.'

Roald still possessed a remarkable ability to understand children in a way many adults never would, and in notes for a lecture that he wrote, but never gave, about what makes a good children's writer, he intended to reveal some of his secrets:

> The writer must have a genuine and powerful wish not only to entertain children, but to teach them the habit of reading. He must be a jokey sort of fellow. He must like simple tricks and jokes and riddles and other childish things. He must be unconventional and inventive. He must know what enthrals children and what bores them. They love chocolates and toys and money. They love being made to giggle. They love seeing the villain meet a grisly death. But they hate descriptive passages and flowery prose. What else do they love? New inventions. Unorthodox methods. Eccentricity. Secret information. The list is long.

He was in constant demand and almost never took a day off, but the bouts of insomnia that had floored him on and off throughout his life returned with a vengeance. Attempting to explain why he found it so hard to sleep, Roald once said he found it almost impossible to switch his brain off when he was busy: 'Your mind is whirring and when you lie down in bed and put the light out, your mind is working on a book all the time,' he explained. 'It's a devastating process actually because you can't get rid of it until you've finished it.'

In January 1990 Liccy was so worried about Roald that she convinced him he was badly in need of a break. He reluctantly agreed to take a rare holiday and they flew to the Caribbean with Liccy's youngest daughter Lorina. They checked into Jamaica Inn – the exclusive colonial lodge where Charles Marsh had persuaded Roald to stick at his marriage to Patricia so many years earlier – and Ophelia met them there. She had been away studying for her degree at Wellesley College in Boston and was delighted to find her father so invigorated after so many health problems. They sat together inventing stories about the other hotel guests, and Roald seemed to be back to his old self again.

But during the trip 26-year-old Lorina, then a glamorous fashion editor at *Harper's* magazine, complained of headaches and a buzzing in her ear. Roald summoned a doctor who diagnosed an ear infection and prescribed antibiotics, and she flew straight to South Africa for a magazine photo shoot. Lorina had no idea that she was in fact suffering from an aggressive brain tumour, and following a sudden aneurysm, she died at the airport. In a hideous twist of fate, Roald's family had been damned by brain injuries yet again. Liccy's older daughter Charlotte said: 'He sort of blamed himself. It was the last straw. He felt a curse had struck again.'

Liccy was inconsolable, and Roald hated being unable to soothe her distress. When she said the only thing she wanted was to be buried next to her daughter, all Roald could think to do was immediately buy the next six plots in the graveyard. Lorina's tragically early death was a brutal reminder to Roald of losing Olivia and he was consumed by grief once again. He slumped into a physical decline from which he never quite recovered.

Roald was suffering from sideroblastic anemia which left him with blurred vision. It was kept at bay with steroids and the regular blood transfusions he endured as part of an experimental new procedure involving having half a pint of blood drained from his eyes twice a week to relieve the pressure; although it seemed to be working, it left him aching and feeble. Any strength he had left, Roald would spend working.

In the aftermath of Lorina's death, painfully reminded that life is short, he vowed to complete various unfinished projects before it was too late. He published a railway safety guide, a nostalgic cookbook of his favourite family recipes, two adult fables and his last short stories for children, *The Minpins* and *Esio Trot*.

Even after fifty years, writing still excited him and what kept Roald going was his belief that no matter how old he got, he still felt like a child, and his Peter Pan like view of the world made everything he tackled feel like a fresh adventure: 'Nothing can prevent the old fires of excitement rekindling once I am well into a story or book. The momentum gathers and the drive towards the last pages becomes as relentless as ever,' he said.

Determine to prove he was not too old to try something new, Roald unexpectedly produced an endearing love story – *Esio Trot* was one of the few tales he ever wrote without any wicked or grotesque characters. There were no villains and no children either, and many of his closest friends thought he had based the ingenious love-struck hero Mr Hoppy on himself. Mr Hoppy, who had been in love with his neighbour Mrs Silver for years, devised an imaginative way to encourage her to reciprocate his feelings. He created a magic spell to make her pet tortoise grow, and told her to recite it daily while secretly replacing each tortoise with a bigger one every few days without her noticing. The whimsical story was a sign that Roald was at last mellowing with age, although he would not agree:

The curious thing is that although I am strictly speaking an old man, I find it impossible to think of myself as being in the least bit ancient. My body may be rusting to pieces, but my mind is something absolutely separate and is as young as ever. I believe that mentally I am a sort of overgrown child, a giggler, a lover of childish jokes and knock knocks, a chocolate and sweet eater, a person with half of him that has failed completely to grow up.

He returned to his usual form with *The Minpins*. His final throw of the dice was the story of a mischievous child who discovered a race of tiny people who helped him destroy a monster in The Forest of Sin. It was in many ways reminiscent of Roald's early wartime stories about the Gremlins. Like the Gremlins, the Minpins wore suction boots when they were above ground, but instead of flying on Hurricanes and Spitfires they hitched rides on the backs of birds. Ophelia recalled that her father had told her a bedtime story years earlier about swallowing a tiny pink pill that made you small enough to ride on the back of a budgerigar. It was the first time since meeting Quentin Blake that Roald had asked for another illustrator, and many saw the story as a poetic farewell from Roald – particularly when the great white swan took Billy on one mysterious final flight, which was seen as a metaphor for death. The lake where they ended up was seen as heaven, and the swans as angels. At that moment in the story it was time for Billy to leave childhood behind and face the drab world of adolescence, and Roald was preoccupied for months with getting the wording exactly as he wanted it:

> Swans glided slowly round and round above this massive crater and then right down into it. Deeper and deeper they went into the dark hole. Suddenly there was a brightness like sunlight below them, and Little Billy could see a vast lake of water, gloriously blue, and on the surface of the lake thousands of swans were swimming slowly about. The pure white of the swans against the blue of the water was very beautiful.

The time had come for Roald to put his financial affairs in order, and so he set up a partnership called Dahl & Dahl which would give Liccy full control over all his work after his death. He then gathered all the children together and informed them that, apart from various gifts and legacies, they were being cut out of his will. To their horror he announced: 'I'm leaving everything to Liccy. I trust her absolutely to do right by you and to do right by the copyrights, and you must too.' Stunned by this unexpected change of heart Lucy said: 'Suddenly our inheritance had gone to zero and we knew he wasn't going to last more than six months.' When the children told Roald how unhappy they were with his decision he apparently retorted: 'If you don't trust Liccy, you can fuck off!' The children knew the cantankerous old man was not for turning, although in the summer of 1990 he reconciled with Patricia, inviting her back to Gipsy House to celebrate Theo's thirtieth birthday, where she even forgave Liccy and the two women became friends.

Over the next few months Roald was in and out of hospital every few weeks with a series of health scares. His anaemia evolved into a rare and incurable form of leukaemia but it was a mellow and reflective time, in which he showed remarkable good humour. He delighted the staff at the John Radcliffe Hospital by inventing nicknames for all the nurses and showering them with presents. He sent Liccy out to buy them all new clothes in case their own were ruined by blood. 'He held nurses in the highest regard,' Liccy said. 'He was fascinated by the medical world and would have been a doctor if he had not been a writer.' During that final spell in hospital Roald was swamped with cards and gifts from thousands of young well-wishers: 'I've been a bit off colour these last few months,' he told them. 'Feeling sleepy when I shouldn't have been and without that lovely old bubbly energy that drives one to write books and drink gin and chase girls.'

In November Ophelia flew home from Boston and was shocked by her father's drastic decline, he was incontinent and impossibly weak. She arrived back at her apartment two days later to find an urgent message from Lucy saying their father had taken a turn for the worse and had made it very clear he did not want to endure a slow and lingering decline. Ophelia headed straight back to the airport, and when she arrived at his bedside Roald told her: 'I am not frightened of falling off my perch. If Olivia can do it, so can I.'

Over the next few nights he started to hallucinate, talking to his mother and Olivia, and the family argued over whether he should be given morphine which would ease the pain, but could hasten his demise. They all knew he dreaded losing both his physical dignity and his mental clarity. On the night of November 22, Children's Day, Roald finally healed his long-standing rift with Tessa, quietly whispering in her ear that he loved her 'very much indeed'. Later that night he told Ophelia he was thirsty so she peeled a tangerine and let the juice run onto his lips. Roald looked at her and said: 'I'm not frightened. It's just that I will miss you all so much.'

They all knew it was time to let him go. In the early hours of the morning the family played one of his favourite pieces of music, Tchaikovsky's Violin Concerto, and gathered around his bed as a nurse injected a lethal dose of morphine. But as the needle pricked his arm Roald muttered 'Ow, fuck!'

He would have been delighted to know those were the last words he ever spoke.

Chapter Twenty

As Liccy and Ophelia drove home from the hospital together in the early hours of the morning, two white doves appeared from the trees and swooped along beside the car for almost a mile. They both felt as if Roald had sent them. He had made it clear that he was ready to die at the age of 74, and the family had given him the dignified ending he would have wished for. Lucy said later: 'Everyone was fine and I think that's what he needed to know. I felt like he'd cleared his desk. Everything was organised.'

But within hours of his death, the family was besieged with calls from the press; a dark rumour had already begun to swirl that Roald had died of AIDS, and had been living a hedonistic double life until the end. But that was not how Roald would be remembered. His hospital consultant Sir David Weatherall led the first of many thousands of touching tributes that would come pouring in over the coming weeks. He wrote:

> In thirty years of clinical practice I cannot remember ever being so moved or privileged in caring for a patient. Roald was quite unique. I have never seen anyone have such an effect on the medical and nursing staff – the sense of loss was quite extraordinary. I was so glad he retained his extraordinary intellect to the end, and that he died with the calm and dignity which was so important to him.

Many of Roald's closest friends were stunned to hear the news as they had not realised how seriously ill he had been; Quentin Blake was among those who said he thought 'He would go on forever'.

It would be a few weeks before Ophelia could bring herself to go into her father's writing hut, his sanctuary, and the birthplace of all his best-loved works. When she pushed open the door everything was exactly as Roald had left it before he died; cigarette butts, the mug filled with sharpened pencils, the foil ball made from discarded sweet wrappers and on his green baize board was a pad of yellow lined paper, but she was astounded to find he had scrawled on it rough notes sketching out the beginnings of yet more children's stories. One of them began: 'The cleverest man in the world is called Mr Billy Bubbler.' Roald had even added a few drawings, and many of his famously eccentric trademarks. The notes continued:

> He can invent just about anything you want. He has a marvellous workshop full of wheels and wires and buckets of glue and balls of string and huge pots full of thick foaming stuff that gives off smoke in many colours. There are old motorcar tyres, baskets of carrots and electric machines and sewing machines and fizzy drink machines and bath tubs and cow's teeth and rice puddings and old shoes and everything else Mr Bubbler needs to make his wonderful inventions.

He had also left the outline of another incomplete story about a gypsy woman who taught a little girl how to talk to her dog, as well as an intriguing idea about characters that only come alive when a child reads the book.

Although his body had been giving up, clearly Roald's imagination was showing no signs of slowing down, and there would have been many more books if only he had the strength to write them. Stephen Roxburgh was convinced that Roald had ideas for at least twenty more untold tales when he died. But towards the end Roald found the process of producing books surprisingly draining. He said writing them was rather like having children, and publishing them was like saying goodbye when they left home. He felt lost when they had gone, and anxious about whether they would be entertaining enough.

His death made headlines around the world and huge numbers of friends, relatives and fans attended his funeral at St Peter and St Paul's Church in Great Missenden where his family gave him a Viking style send-off in a nod to his Nordic heritage. Roald was buried with many of his favourite objects including his snooker cues, several bottles of Burgundy wine, the Dixon Ticonderoga pencils he always wrote with, a power saw and of course chocolates. To this day children still leave many of the same items, as well as toys and flowers, at his graveside.

The CEO of Penguin Books, Peter Mayer, gave a eulogy paying tribute to Roald's many generous acts of charity and philanthropy, and went on to reveal how supportive he had been in the aftermath of Mayer's controversial decision to publish Salman Rushdie's book *The Satanic Verses*, which led to a fatwa put on the author and death threats for Mayer and his staff. Mayer explained: 'He tried to figure out how I could go forward in what had become a publishing drama. With brains and hearts he wanted to protect me.' Mourners talked fondly of Roald's genius and kindness, as well as his unpredictable and volatile outbursts, which were quickly diffused by his notoriously dark humour.

It seems impossible to imagine now, but Roald only actually won one award for children's fiction in his lifetime; he never achieved the global accolades his work regularly receives today. Since his death however, Roald has been honoured repeatedly in a remarkably varied number of different ways. A few months after the funeral, Liccy's best friend Amanda Conquy left her job in publishing to help run his literary estate which has grown into a wide-ranging and far-reaching legacy of film, theatre, opera, musical and concert adaptations of his work. Liccy has opened numerous popular attractions in Roald's name and founded Roald Dahl's Mavellous Children's Charity, a fundraising organisation to help provide specialist paediatric nurses to thousands of children suffering from brain and blood disorders.

'Roald knew from tragic experience how crucial nurses are,' Liccy explained. 'They are there from the moment of diagnosis, an extremely frightening and lonely time for both the child and the parents, a moment I have experienced as a parent myself. Neurology has been a big thing in the family. We have been hit in every direction.'

The charity is the legacy closest to Roald's heart as he had always been moved to help sick children. He campaigned tirelessly for the widespread uptake of the measles vaccine when it became available. Liccy added: 'Because of all the desperate tragedies he had been through, he never gave up. He always said that this child, this adult, could be saved. There had to be a way.'

In 1996 the Roald Dahl Children's Gallery was opened at the Buckinghamshire County Museum in Aylesbury and the Czech astronomer Antonin Mrkos discovered a new main-belt asteroid which was named the 6223 Dahl in his honour.

Matilda was adapted into a successful film starring Danny DeVito, and later into a hit West End musical which has since gone on to be performed around the world, winning dozens of theatrical awards.

In 2002 the Oval Basin Plaza in Cardiff was renamed the Roald Dahl Plass, using the Norwegian word for square, and in 2005 the Roald Dahl Museum and Story Centre was opened in Great Missenden – a hugely popular tourist attraction which is visited by well over 50,000 visitors from around the world every year. In 2003 four of his books appeared in a nationwide survey by the BBC to discover Britain's best-loved novel of all time. The Royal Society of Literature included *Charlie and the Chocolate Factory* in a list of ten books every child should read, and Roald ranked in sixteenth place on *The Times* list of The 50 Greatest British Writers since 1945. In 2008 the former Children's Laureate Michael Rosen launched the Roald Dahl Funny Prize, which is awarded every year for humorous children's fiction; and in September 2009 a blue plaque was unveiled by Liccy and Theo in his honour in his Welsh birthplace Llandaff. But rather than installing the plaque on the wall of the house where he was actually born, they chose to have it on the wall of the former sweet shop where Roald had devised the Great Mouse Plot of 1924 that featured so prominently in his first autobiography *Boy*.

The School Library Journal, a publication with a primarily American readership, included four of Roald's books in its shortlist of the all-time best children's novels and the same year a set of stamps were issued by Royal Mail featuring Quentin Blake's most recognisable illustrations for *Charlie and the Chocolate Factory, The Twits, The Witches, Matilda, Fantastic Mr Fox* and *James and the Giant Peach*.

In 2005 director Tim Burton cast Hollywood actor Johnny Depp as Willy Wonka in a remake of *Charlie and the Chocolate Factory*, fourteen years after plans for the film had started. Other famous film stars including Bill Murray and Jim Carrey had been considered for the iconic role but it had languished in development until 1998 when Liccy and Lucy were given total artistic control over the choosing of the cast, director and scriptwriter. They chose Tim Burton after he visited Gipsy House and the moment he walked into Roald's writing hut he exclaimed: 'This is the Bucket's house!' Liccy remembered thinking, 'Thank God, somebody gets it.' Depp's portrayal of Wonka as a bizarre, reclusive germophobe with an oddly high pitched voice led many to suggest he had based the character on the singer Michael Jackson. The film was a huge hit, grossing $475 million worldwide and *Charlie and The Chocolate Factory* soared back into the New York Times bestseller list from July to October 2005.

A stop-motion animated film version of *Fantastic Mr Fox* was released in 2009, starring George Clooney and Meryl Streep as the voices of Mr and Mrs Fox. Directed by Wes Anderson, this film also suffered a number of delays and had been in production for five years.

When 'the Olympic Games were held in London in 2012 and artist Sir Peter Blake was asked to select British cultural icons to recreate his famous *Sgt Peppers Lonely Hearts Club Band* album cover, Roald was among his first choices. He was also featured among The New Elizabethans, a list of people 'whose actions during the reign of Elizabeth II have had a significant impact on lives in these islands and given the age its character', chosen to mark the Queen's Diamond Jubilee.

In 2016, to mark the centenary of Roald's birth, Dr Susan Rennie compiled *The Oxford Roald Dahl Dictionary* which included many of his invented words from The BFG and their implied meanings. She commented that some of Roald's words have already escaped his world into everyday English, such as *Scrumdiddlyumptious*, meaning food that is utterly delicious. The BFG was eventually released as a feature length film that year after more than twenty years in development. Paramount Pictures first acquired the film rights in 1991, and comedian Robin Williams was lined up to play the title role in 1998, but when his famous improvisational style clashed with the book's unique language, the script lingered in the early stages of development for so long that the film rights reverted back to Roald's estate. In 2011 DreamWorks acquired the film rights and three years later, with Steven Spielberg at the helm, the film went into production. Shakespearean actor Mark Rylance, who had worked with Spielberg on his award winning film *Bridge of Spies* agreed to take on the role of the giant using motion capture filming, but when it was released box office takings were low, the reviews were generally negative and it proved to be one of the least profitable films of Spielberg's career.

In 2016 *Revolting Rhymes*, Roald's humorous re-interpretation of well-known nursery rhymes and fairy tales was produced as a two part animated film starring a host of British actors including Dominic West and Rob Brydon, and was later nominated for an Oscar.

Some of the letters Roald sent to his mother over the years were broadcast as BBC Radio 4's *Book of the Week*, and in 2017 Roald was named the greatest storyteller of all time, ranking ahead of Shakespeare, Dickens and J. K. Rowling. Scores of celebrities and film makers have credited Roald with inspiring their work; comedian David Walliams, whose stories are often compared to his, said: 'He is the Master. The best you can hope for is to learn from him. I can appreciate how truly brilliant Dahl was – I can admire the economy with which he writes. He is totally in control of his narrative at every point.'

Roald now ranks among the world's bestselling fiction authors with sales of well over 250 million, and his books published in sixty languages, from Serbian to Mandarin; every year on 13 September his birthday is celebrated not only in Britain and America, but across Africa, Australia and South America too.

Looking back at his legacy, a century after his birth, Roald still has a splintered reputation. He created some of the greatest and most memorable characters in literary history, from the legend that is Willy Wonka, to Matilda and Sophie, the orphaned bookworms who are heroines to millions of girls to this day.

Roald Dahl has achieved 'national treasure' status since his death, but the man was a gobblefunk of contradictions. He may have been just as rotsome as his worst monsters and it is that magical blend of marvellous and revolting that made him and his books so very squiff-squigglingly swashboggling.